OWNING THE MAT

THE MAKING OF A STATE CHAMPION OR AT LEAST A GOOD MAN

"Dan Blanchard and Brian Preece do it again with another interesting wrestling book."- Dan Gable

AUTHORS: DAN BLANCHARD & BRIAN PREECE

Hey Coach!

This is my third book— more stories about my coaching and wrestling for my Dad. You, David & Harry and my Dad were legends. I very much enjoy your Facebook Posts about your exploits and adventures! Happy Holidays!

Brian
Preece

TALE OF CONTENTS

FOREWORD 1

INTRODUCTION 5

ENDORSEMENTS 7

CHAPTER 1: The Final Year of Dakota's Journey Begins 16

CHAPTER 2: Dakota's High School Program Saved from Being Eliminated 30

CHAPTER 3: Facing and Overcoming Doubt 43

CHAPTER 4: Still Wrestling with COVID-19................................57

CHAPTER 5: 'This Too Shall Pass' and 'The Sun Will Come up Tomorrow'.. 66

CHAPTER 6: Bad Weather and COVID-19 Rearing Their Ugly Heads in Connecticut..76

CHAPTER 7: A Time to Reflect on the Good Things Wrestling Brings 85

CHAPTER 8: Great Wrestling Coaches May Pass Away but Their Legend Never Dies 94

CHAPTER 9: Being There After a Tough Loss.............................106

CHAPTER 10: Learning Life Lessons from Losses on the Mat....120

CHAPTER 11: No "Senior Night" for Dakota 133

CHAPTER 12: Gutting it Out!.....................................141

CHAPTER 13: Having an Attitude of Gratitude as Dakota's High School Season Ends 156

CHAPTER 14: In Dakota's Own Words 174

ABOUT THE AUTHORS..183

FOREWORD

When Dan Blanchard first asked me to write the Foreword for the third book of his wrestling trilogy with Brian Preece. I was both extremely honored and equally terrified. I am not a writer and don't want to lower the standards of their amazing book series. However, the wrestler in me doesn't quit or is afraid to fail!! So I decided to give it my best effort, which is all anyone can ever do.

I first met Dan playing Pop Warner football in middle school. I later convinced him to give wrestling a try. Dan was an exceptional athlete, extremely strong, had great balance, and took to wrestling like a fish to water. All these years late, I am fortunate enough to know Dan's son, Dakota. I have known him since the day he was born. Time has a way of playing tricks with your mind. There are days when it seems like Dakota was born yesterday; other times, it feels like lifetimes ago.

I was elated when Dan and Dakota showed up at my wrestling club KT Kidz four years ago. As I have previously eluded, Dan was a fantastic wrestler. He was also a great drilling partner and a better friend. Whenever I was training for a tournament, I would always seek Dan out at whichever high school he was coaching to sneak in a few workouts with him. So, I knew that

Dakota had the potential to be very good, if not great, like his father.

Fortunately for me, Dakota came to me as a blank slate. So I was excited to be able to mold him in the way I thought would be best for him to be successful. Dakota had participated in various sports throughout elementary and middle school, but this would be his first time on the mat. Having never wrestled, he didn't have any bad habits or techniques I would have to erase before we could build. Dan had shared that Dakota's life had been relatively easy up to this point, so he was a bit worried about how Dakota would respond to the rigors of wrestling. Especially to getting beat up on the wrestling mat.

I saw nothing but raw talent and toughness from that first practice from Dakota. He had these elastic shoulders that frustrated some of my more experienced wrestlers in the room when they would crank a half-nelson on him, and Dakota refused to go to his back. I was very impressed with Dakota, and I let Dan know it. I even joked with them that perhaps Dakota was a better athlete than his old man. I was looking forward to seeing how good Dakota could be.

I felt so grateful to be a small part of the father and son's journey of chasing a state championship. Fully knowing that the road ahead was paved with many difficulties but having confidence that becoming a good man with the help of my beloved sport of wrestling, the oldest and toughest sport known to humankind, was a sure thing.

To me, wrestling is a microcosm of life. In wrestling, you can do all of the "right things," eat clean, lift weights, drill to perfection, and run. You can push yourself to and past limits that you once thought were unobtainable and still lose to someone better than you. You don't always get your way much like life, and sometimes it's not fair.

But what wrestling teaches you is to get back up and do it again. To learn from your failures, use them as motivation, and work harder. Wrestling humbles you like nothing else. It's just you out there, no team to help, nowhere to hide, just YOU and somebody who wants to beat the tar out of you.

Those with the most success learn very quickly that there are no excuses. All of your failures are yours and yours alone. You have to look in the mirror and hold yourself accountable to be successful. It's never easy. But you grow from the pain.

What defines a wrestler? Is it how many wins they have? How many medals or trophies they win? Have they won a state title? To me, it's none of those. It's how you respond to defeat. Do you battle back and take third, or quit on yourself. Life will be very hard at times. You need to pick yourself up and fight back. I wish Dakota lived closer to my club. And I wish Dan didn't have to work so many jobs. Those two factors kept me from seeing and coaching Dakota as much as I would have liked that first fall season of Dakota's high school wrestling career.

After that fall preseason, Dakota began his freshman year at E.O. Smith High School. I didn't get to see much of him during his first wrestling season, but I did keep tabs on him. I kept up to speed on Dakota's progress through countless calls with Dan and reading his new wrestling blog, which later became the wrestling book, *Hitting the Mat, which* he and Brian Preece co-wrote. It seemed like Dakota was a natural, having instant success and getting better each week. And he might have a chance, against all odds, of becoming a state champion by his senior year.

Sadly, Dakota only lasted one day with me at my fall practices his sophomore year due to a knee problem. Unfortunately, that problem persisted, and he needed surgery and lost his entire sophomore season. Additionally, due to the COVID-19 pandemic that shut down the state of Connecticut for 18 months, he missed out on his junior season as well. Poor kid couldn't catch a break.

Then I had to move. I wished Dakota and Dan the best at my going away party. Poway Regional Olympic Training Center in California hired me as their new head coach. I knew it would be difficult for Dakota to reach his first goal of becoming a state champ, considering how much wrestling he has missed. But, regarding his other goal of becoming a good man, I was confident that he was already well on his way to achieving that one. No one or nothing was going to deny him. I was sad that I wouldn't see much of Dakota's senior year of wrestling because of my new job across the country. But, I was also delighted to know that I would still know what was going on through Dan's blog and the next wrestling book Dan and Brian were writing.

In conclusion, I don't want to give away the end of this book here at the beginning of it by telling you if Dakota becomes a state champion or not. But, I will tell you he's well on his way to becoming a good man through man's oldest sport, and I couldn't be prouder of Dakota. I also cherish my friendship with his father, my old friend, and fellow wrestling teammate, Dan Blanchard. I know the wrestling community is going to love this book!

John Knapp-

**Head Coach of Poway Olympic
Regional Training Center**

INTRODUCTION

Dan Blanchard and Brian Preece's third book, *Owning the Mat: The Making of a State Champ or At Least A Good Man* is a wonderful wrestling read for wrestlers, and their families, alike. I met Dan in the summer of 1986 when he attended my Boston University Wrestling Camp. Dan won the camp tournament with five pins. Years ago at another camp I did, I met former West High School head coach Don Holtry, who worked with Brian for five years in helping build trophy winning teams in the 1990s . I am happy that Don and Brian were able to incorporate some of the techniques in their program.

Dan and Brian are two very different men who both adore the sport of wrestling and produce good young men who become good men who give back to their communities. And this is exactly what Dan and Brian are trying to do for Dakota. They offer their words of wisdom and encouragement and their writings in this book and the two previous ones.

In this third book, Dakota is finally a senior and in his last year of high school wrestling. After much debate, Connecticut opened back up its wrestling programs and moved forward with Covid protocols in place. *Owning the Mat* chronicles the ups and downs of Dakota's final high school wrestling season. The pandemic, injuries, illness, and New England weather cause a lot of stops and starts in Dakota's last season, which is filled with a lot of highs and lows for both Dakota and his father, Daniel.

I don't want to give away the ending of the story of whether or not Dakota does reach his goal of becoming a high school wrestling champion. But, what I can tell you is that in Dan and Brian's writings, one feels like they are right there in the middle of the action with Dakota in Connecticut. And contributing to the richness of the book coming from out west in Utah, Brian and his stories of his legendary father-coach and the many greats who have come out of Utah over the years wonderfully compliments Dakota's journey.

Dakota, you have obviously developed into a fine young man and a pretty good wrestler, too, from the stories that your father and Brian share in this book. Great job. I have no doubt that wrestling helped make you a better young man. And I know that whatever you set your mind on next, you will do well.

Maybe Dan and Brian still have another book in them after this one.

Readers, get ready for a great story, the journey of a hero story when you open up this book and venture in between the book covers of this fantastic coming-of-age wrestling book

Carl Adams

Wrestling Hall of Famer

ENDORSEMENTS

Dan Blanchard and Brian Preece do it again with another very interesting book that caps off Dakota's storybook high school wrestling career.

These two excellent coaches, fathers and men tell a tale of Dakota's journey through wrestling, where we're all reminded of hard life and wrestling can be.

Dakota overcomes one injury after another plus Covid 19 to make it the State Tournament, where he plans on winning a State Championship and further cement his role as a good young man.

This book is a fun read and a straightforward way to step inside the world of wrestling or anything tough to conquer.

Anyone associated with a pursuit of excellence will enjoy this book and walk away with some insights into the real world and how to become successful.

Dan Gable
Olympic Champion
Championship Coach
Iowa Athlete of the Century

As I said in Dan Blanchard's and Brian Preece's previous book, this wrestling story of Dakota facing nonstop adversity has the makings of something great. Dakota has had one obstacle after another thrown in his way throughout his high school wrestling career, finally culminating in his appearance in the State Championships. Once again, Dan and Brian do a great job in this final book of their trilogy. They continue to share their past stories of wrestling and coaching with a steady eye on Dakota's journey toward a state championship. I won't spoil the ending here on whether or not Dakota reaches his goal of becoming a state champion. Still, I will share that he has made incredible progress in becoming a good man through man's oldest sport.

Lee Kemp
4X NCAA Finalists
4X World Champion
Youngest American World Champion
Hall of Famer

In this third book by Dan Blanchard and Brian Preece, Dakota continues to fight to find a way to learn and grow among the setbacks that just don't seem to ever stop for him. Dakota's father, coach, and former standout wrestler, Dan Blanchard, tells another beautiful story of perseverance. We find ourselves rooting for Dakota and the obtainment of his goal of winning a state championship. And once again, we see Brian Preece complimenting each tale Dan tells about Dakota with his own wealth of knowledge and experience in coming from the great wrestling state of Utah and being the son of one of its greatest coaches, Dennis Preece. Buy this book right now. It will inspire you both on and off the mat to overcome adversity and become the best possible version of yourself.

Ben Kjar
UVU's First NCAA DIV I All-American

Daniel Blanchard and Brian Preece have written a must-read for any wrestling parent or fan! Read this book and learn the emotions of Dan, a parent/coach, as he passes along his passion for wrestling and life through lessons to his son, Dakota, and everyone he comes in contact with during Dakotas senior season of high school- learn lessons from one of the best as they navigate through the ups and downs of a COVID season.

Scott Legacy
Head Wrestling Coach Castleton University

"Owning the Mat" is a beautiful wrestling story that mimics the hero's journey that we all love. Dakota is a high school wrestler going into his senior year. His goal is to become a state champ. Dakota has had adversity after adversity chronicled in the wrestling books his father/coach Dan Blanchard and Brian Preece, the son of a legendary coach, have written about Dakota's journey through all the ups and downs of wrestling. If you are a wrestler or a wrestling family, you must read this book. It will warm your heart and inspire your soul all at the same time.

Steven H. Fraser
Olympic Gold Medalist and Wrestling Coach

In whatever ways one is involved in wrestling, this book, "Owning the Mat," offers another great inside peek into the high school wrestling world. The back and forth dialogue of Brian Preece and Dan Blanchard is terrific and fun. Dan, the dad/coach of his son Dakota, is pushing hard to help his son Dakota reach his goal to become a state champ in his final season. And once again, Brian continues to deftly enrich the wrestling story of Dan and Dakota with his own wonderful dialogue from a perspective of a son of a legendary Utah wrestling coach. I wholeheartedly encourage you to read this wrestling book. You won't be sorry. And you'll even learn a thing or two from this inside peek into man's oldest and most demanding sport shared by two men doing their best to help Dakota do his best.

Jeff Newby
Executive Director of USA Wrestling Utah

Dan Blanchard and Brian Preece continue to guide us through life's hard-learned lessons by observing, participating in, and recording Dakota's journey to becoming a state champ wrestler and a good man during his senior year of high school. Dakota continues to face one obstacle after another, including a pandemic that won't go away. So many kids, parents, coaches, and athletes will relate to the struggle of training during Covid and what Dakota has endured. Brian and Dan help contribute to Dakota and show how the entire wrestling community embodies a can-do attitude in order to face any of life's challenges. You're going to want to get this book and find out if Dakota reached his goal of winning a state championship and becoming a good man.

Katherine Shai
Eight-Time U.S. National Team member

What a wonderful concluding read "Owning the Mat" is for anyone associated with wrestling. Find out if Dakota's senior year season ends with him reaching his goal of becoming a state champ and a good man. Once again, there are a lot of great wrestlers speaking in this book. And the dual perspectives of Dan Blanchard and Brian Preece continue to be very interesting and insightful. Dan, the former champion wrestler, gives all he has to help his son Dakota become a state champ. And Brian Preece, who wrestled for his father, one of Utah's greatest coaches, has teamed up with Dan again to write another excellent wrestling book. This is another book that opens the door of wrestling for all to come on inside, make oneself comfortable as a dear friend, and root for the wrestlers and their families all over this great nation of ours. I don't think you'll want to miss out on Dan and Brian's third and final wrestling book. Pick up a copy right now and step right into the amazing and enriching world of high school wrestling.

Terry Davis
Author of *Vision Quest* Book Turned Movie

Once again, Dan Blanchard and his son Dakota's journey through the ups and downs of the wrestling world continues. I have grown close to Dakota, and his dad/coach Dan Blanchard and coauthor Brian Preece in the wrestling trilogy the three of them have created. Like their previous two books, "Hitting the Mat" and "Trying to Take the Mat," this book, "Owning the Mat," continues to give one an amazing inside peek into the arduous journey of wrestling. This is another excellent book on developing personal excellence. You should pick it up right now.

John Bennett
World Champ
Hall of Fame

"Owning the Mat" is a perfect ending to the wrestling trilogy book series Dan Blanchard and Brian Preece have put together on Dakota's journey as a high school wrestler. Dakota's senior year is no exception to the highs and lows that every wrestler goes through. Wrestlers and wrestling families will enjoy this book. Way to go, Dakota, on working extremely hard to chase your dreams of becoming a state champ and a good man.

Anibal Nieves
All-American
2X Olympian

A wonderful story of the journey of a father and son toward a lifelong goal. This book will give a very unique look into that journey. But, more importantly, the love and bond between a father and son. And how the pursuit of that goal affects that relationship and, ultimately, the results of their pursuit. You will be inspired and amazed at what the sport of wrestling did for this duo and what it can do for you. Enjoy.

Kerry McCoy
2X NCAA Champion
2X Olympian

Facing adversity is a way of life. Earning the right to succeed doesn't always come with a guarantee that it will happen. Putting your best foot forward is what Dakota did to achieve his goal in "Owning the Mat." Like Dakota, when you push yourself hard and believe in yourself, there are no limits to what you can do. Whether you win or learn, you never lose in the sport of wrestling. If you lose a match or a situation during the match, don't lose the lesson it taught you. If you learn something from it, it is a huge win both in sports and life. Persevering through injuries and adversity makes us stronger and better people for working through it. I admire Dakota's perseverance and goals to climb to the top in this book. This is a good wrestling book. Enjoy it. I did.

Mean Gene Mills
Olympian and World Super Champion

Dan Blanchard and Brian Preece's unique father-son perspective through the sport of wrestling based on Dakota's high school wrestling career is finally reaching an end in this third wrestling book of the trilogy, "Owning the Mat." In Dakota's senior year, nothing has gotten any easier. Dakota continues to have a lot of ups and downs, which is expected in the sport of wrestling. The highs and lows intensify when it's one's senior year. And Dakota is still battling injuries, a pandemic, New England weather, and referee calls that just don't go the way he and his dad wants them to. This book is another beautiful example of a teen boy coming to age in man's oldest sport. It is a must-read for wrestling families.

Ken Chertow
Olympian

Another great wrestling story of the father-coach and son-wrestler journey in this coming-of-age quest to make Dakota a good man through his struggles in the sport of high school wrestling. Like life, there are many ups and downs and twists and triumphs and heartbreaks. You're going to really enjoy this book.

Carl Poff
Hall of Fame Wrestling Coach Lock Haven University

Another great wrestling book by the dual Dan Blanchard and Brian Preece. This third book of their wrestling trilogy cumulates with Dakota's last shot at winning a high school state championship and his last shot to further build his character as a good man as a high school wrestler. The book catches one's interest authentically and doesn't let up until the referee blows the final whistle in the state tournament. Any family involved in wrestling will enjoy this book.

Mike Foy
2X Olympian
Wrestling Coach

Chapter 1

THE FINAL YEAR OF DAKOTA'S JOURNEY BEGINS

Dan Blanchard: It's hard to believe how fast time flies. We're already in the preseason of my son Dakota's senior year of high school wrestling and his quest to become a state champ or at least a good man. Furthermore, Brian Preece, my co-author, and I are also now co-creating the third book of our wrestling book series that began with Dakota's freshman year of wrestling with, *Hitting the Mat.* Dakota's high school wrestling career is almost over, and so is his shot at reaching his goals and using high school wrestling to become a good man.

While in the pandemic lockdown, nobody was wrestling anywhere around us in Connecticut. Fortunately, though, we received a stimulus check that gave us the ability to buy a small 10X10 basement wrestling mat. It isn't big enough for us to go full speed on. But it is big enough for us to do some drilling, mat wrestling, and stretching on. So, we were pretty pumped about getting the home wrestling mat to continue my son Dakota's journey of becoming a good man by trying to become a state champ wrestler.

However, nothing is ever simple in life. After a few weeks, the delivery came. But only half of the wrestling mat showed up. We had one 5X10 section of the mat. The other half of the mat was lost in the mail. We were frustrated and reached out to Amazon. They refunded us and told us we could keep that one mat section and order another one.

So, I went down in the basement and moved a few more things over to make additional room for three 5X10 sections of the mat instead of just two of them. Maybe this was a blessing in disguise. The downside is that the new 10X10 mat that we just ordered would take a few months to arrive because everyone was bombarding Amazon with their stimulus check spending. And various events around the world were slowing down the circulation of products like that huge boat stuck in the Suez Canal.

Over the next few months, Dakota and I did the best we could on our new tiny 5X10 one-section mat to get a workout and some technique in. We did a bunch of light drilling but had to be really careful not to fall off the mat onto the hard concrete floor.

Eventually, the other mat showed up, and Dakota and I were pumped! My four daughters were happy, too. They used the wrestling mat for some aerobics training around Dakota's drilling sessions with me. Unfortunately, though, almost as soon as we got the mat, my shoulder hit the wrestling mat funny when Dakota took me down. And I heard it crack three times, and it sent shooting pains all over my body. So, we had to immediately stop. I couldn't do any more wrestling that day. That shoulder injury haunted me for the next few months, not allowing Dakota and me to take full advantage of our new wrestling mat.

Also, Dakota had an ongoing elbow injury for the last few months that just wouldn't go away. So, that too made it harder for us to take full advantage of our newfound luck of having a wrestling mat in our basement. Sadly, injuries and the pandemic continued to plague our progress in man's oldest and most demanding sport.

Neither Dakota nor I seemed able to shake our injuries, so we decided to take some time off from working out to let our bodies heal. However, as Murphy's Law states, if something can go wrong, it will. On Dakota's first day back working out, he did a light trail run, and unfortunately, Dakota's foot came down wrong, and he heard it crack. I brought him to the doctor, hoping it wasn't broken. Thankfully it wasn't. He just sprained it. But now, he needed a few more weeks off to let his ankle heal.

After a few weeks off, Dakota's ankle seemed well enough for us to do some light drilling again on our new basement mat. Immediately, my heel flared up and gave me a lot of pain. My heel had been bugging me the previous few weeks, and it nagged me for the next few months. I wondered if Dakota would be better off with a much younger drilling partner than myself. Also, within the next couple of workouts, it became apparent that there was still something very wrong with Dakota's elbow.

I finally gave in and brought Dakota to the doctor to look at his elbow. The doctor said that he had severely sprained his elbow to the point of dislocation while wrestling a while back. And that Dakota had not given it the proper amount of time to heal.

The doctor told Dakota to cease all upper body physical activity for six weeks, including wrestling.

Dang! We were fortunate enough to get a new home wrestling mat because of the stimulus money. And now, one thing after another keeps us from taking advantage of it. However, I always try to look on the bright side of things. So, I told Dakota not to worry about it. Better to take time off now for an injury than during the wrestling season. With this injury happening in the late spring, he had plenty of time to heal and still get in good shape before the wrestling season started on the Monday after Thanksgiving here in Connecticut.

We soon learned that there was a Nutmeg Wrestling Tournament scheduled for July 25th at New Britain High School, where I used to teach and coach wrestling. This was awesome. Perfect timing, too. Dakota's six weeks of resting his elbow ended when we'd return from our family summer vacation. And we would still have two weeks for Dakota to train for the tournament and get in shape. We were pumped over this stroke of luck. It has been a very long time since Dakota has wrestled competitively,

As soon as we got back from vacation, Dakota and I went into training. On the third day of his training, I went online to register him for the tournament when I found out that the facility decided to keep the mask mandate in place until the end of the summer. Thus, the wrestling tournament was canceled.

The pandemic had struck again. And once again, Dakota is stuck standing on the sidelines just watching his high school years pass by without him competing. He hasn't competed in the sport of wrestling since his freshman year. And it's becoming very frustrating. But I guess that's how life is sometimes, right?

Well, at least Dakota and I were able to get some more drilling in while we're waiting to see what will happen next in the new Covid and wrestling world. However, we had to slam on the brakes in Dakota's training again because I now had Lyme disease. But, in about a month, it looked like my Lyme disease and the blotches it had left all over my body had cleared up, and Dakota and I resumed training. But these training sessions were a bit painful for Dakota because he was now dealing with an ingrown toenail. Ah, there is always something, huh? We both keep getting these damn painful pebbles in our shoes as we try to walk through our lives toward more success on the wrestling mats.

Finally, everything seemed to be in place, and both Dakota and I were healthy. We were back into training on our new basement wrestling mat, and everything seemed great until my arm got caught in Dakota's loose shirt right as he hit a move on me. My elbow popped, and my tricep tore. We couldn't seem to win. There was a never-ending one thing after another holding us back from making progress.

But we refused to be beaten. And it's a good thing, too, because this was when Jude Knapp, Johnny's younger brother, and I talked on the phone. Jude told me KT Wrestling was opening back up, and Dakota should come down there to wrestle. I thought that was a great idea. Dakota could finally wrestle with someone besides me and occasionally Shirzad, who Dakota has gotten a little too big for.

Even though KT KIDZ was an hour's drive away, it was awesome. It was exactly what Dakota needed for his fall training with me laid up with a bad elbow and torn tricep. Dakota had a successful fall season of wrestling with KT KIDZ. However, life continued to be crazy because Dakota injured cartilage in his chest near the end of the fall season, causing his chest to pop continuously and painfully. And to make matters worse, then we found out that his high school head wrestling coach took another job, and Dakota might not have a head coach or even a high school team to go back to. Life is crazy!

Earlier in my life, I didn't realize what I would say next when I was a wrestler, two-time state champ, and two-time Junior Olympian in high school. But I understand it now. Okay. Here it is. Are you ready for it? It's almost a damn miracle for a kid to win the States...

Well, regardless, we're going to reach for that miracle anyway. And if Dakota fails to capture that miracle, he'll at least build his character and become a good man who knows how to work hard and come back from setbacks. And that's all anyone can ask of him. Wouldn't you agree?

Brian Preece: Welcome back to the third installment in our trilogy following Dakota's wrestling career. After a promising freshman season, the past two years have seen nothing but frustration for Dakota. He has dealt with a bevy of injuries, and then the state of Connecticut canceled high school sports his entire junior year. Now Dakota is getting healthier and wants to get to the top of the podium his senior year. But as Daniel described, there is still a lot of uncertainty. My role here is to add my own insights and stories from my coaching years and wrestling for my father, one of the most successful high school coaches in our nation's history. But as I said in the first book, our coaching journey was far from smooth.

Daniel is doing everything he can to get Dakota mat time, even purchasing a wrestling mat for the basement. Even though my father was a championship wrestling coach, and we had room in the basement of both the houses I lived in, we never had a mat. It wasn't that my Mom thought a wrestling mat would ruin the downstairs decor; I don't think my Dad wanted one either. My Dad wanted to compartmentalize his life a bit and come home and leave the wrestling world on the mat at school if he could.

And when he coached at Uintah High School in Vernal, a small town near the Utah/Colorado border, he was very involved in the Little League program. So he would come home during wrestling season very late at night as he would have the high school wrestling practice and then run the Little League practices after that. Beyond that, the high school was within walking distance, and my Dad had keys to the building.

When we moved from Vernal to Salt Lake City, I was in the sixth grade and showing signs of burnout. I did a lot of weekend freestyle tournaments somewhat against my will. But at the same time, wrestling was what I was best at. I developed my own unique wrestling style, and with some experience, I did okay. One or two kids always seemed to beat me in these freestyle tournaments. But in junior high, I did manage to win the district championship of twelve or so schools from the middle of Salt Lake valley.

When I got to junior high, there was a short junior high folkstyle season, and after that, there was the weekend freestyle season for grades K-12. It was the latter I was getting sick of. My Dad would also drag me down to the Sundance Wrestling Club run by Jeff Winderlin, a great wrestling mind, and a good guy. It was not him in any way why I didn't want to go on Tuesday and Thursday nights for extra practice. I was just sick of wrestling. Plus, there was my friend David Lucero, who I call the best wrestler Utah had in the 1980s. I know opinions will vary, but he's the only Utah high school wrestler I know of that had an undefeated career in high school competition. Not even Cael Sanderson did that in our state. Lucero won "just" two state titles. In our school district, freshmen weren't allowed to compete in high school competitions, and academic issues prevented him from wrestling at region and state his sophomore season. But he would have won four titles, and there's no doubt in anyone's mind who saw him wrestle. But why I brought up David was because, in junior high, we were actually the same size, and he threw me around like a rag doll. And he often sought me out to throw me like a rag doll. And even though we were friends then, and still friends now, his wrestling prowess didn't really make me want to be there. It's not that fun counting the lights.

I continued to go to a lot of freestyle meets in seventh and eighth grade, but after my ninth-grade year, I just told my Dad I was done. I would wrestle for my school, which I generally enjoyed, but I just wanted a break from the off-season stuff. I maybe got talked into a couple of meets here or there, and most of the time, I brought home medals. But I remember when I lost to this one kid who was basically a novice and didn't even have wrestling shoes, my Dad (and Mom) were livid. My lack of effort was very noticeable. I guess this is when I "quit" wrestling for the very first time.

I was actually decent at basketball, and I thought maybe I might give that a try in high school. In our school district at the time, junior high was grades seven through nine, so as I entered my sophomore year, I really thought about trying out for the team. I was probably good enough to make a sophomore team with 15-20 players of my own grade on the roster. But I wasn't good enough to filter through until my senior year. Maybe deep down, I realized that. I did golf on the high school team my sophomore year as I guess I had a lot of time to work on my game since my wrestling career was "over."

But it wasn't really over, and when November rolled around, I found myself in the wrestling room. Wrestling, for better or worse, was my identity. However, my sophomore year was rough. And I had my first losing season as a wrestler. But I enjoyed my teammates and really liked our young head coach, Alan Albright. And even with some setbacks, like being the only JV wrestler for a few meets on a team of about ten guys, I finally started to figure things out a bit. I took third in a varsity tournament and upset a ranked kid in a dual meet. Then managed to place fourth in the region (league) to qualify for state, where I won a couple of matches and nearly placed in the top six.

Then my high school coach left, and about two-thirds of our very small team graduated. The school was scrambling to find a coach, much like what was happening with Dakota and his school. Thankfully, my Dad stepped up to do it. But it was hard for my Dad because he wasn't a teacher in the building. I wouldn't say my father was a technique guru, though he knew enough.

His magic was recruiting and promotion, which was simply hard at our school. I also wouldn't say I had a stellar junior season, but I did win our region tournament and placed sixth in state. I think I had like a 16-10 record. Back in those days, we didn't wrestle like our high school kids in Utah do now. They rack up maybe fifty to sixty matches and wrestle in six tournaments plus region (now called divisionals) and state. And some of these tournaments are massive, like the Rockwell Rumble, where there will be 75 or so teams and close to 1000 wrestlers with brackets of over 64 wrestlers in some weights. I actually skied some weekends because we wrestled in maybe four tournaments. One was a 16-team event which we thought was huge, as most of the tourneys were eight-team affairs which were often held over two days. We had our five region dual meets and maybe three or four other pre-season duals. There were byes in some of these tournaments, so maybe I would only get two or three matches, win or lose. Like my sophomore year, I wrestled the best at the end of the season.

The following year we maybe had five or six returning wrestlers and two returning state qualifiers, me and my friend Jon Clark, who also took sixth in state. My parents did a great job respecting my wishes. They didn't even suggest after my sophomore and junior high school seasons to do any extra wrestling. And I was generally willing to oblige. My Dad did a two-day camp/clinic bringing in Bobby Douglas, who might have been the Arizona State coach at that time. I showed up for a couple of sessions, but that was about it. After my sophomore high school season ended in mid-February, I got a job at Dan's Foods, a local supermarket. It was a job I enjoyed. It gave me a good friend group, many of which attended our rival high school Olympus.

But I found myself taking a lot of Saturday shifts, and when I didn't have a Saturday shift, I was up in the mountains doing some spring skiing or playing golf.

After my junior year, I decided to do a little bit more, a little bit more wrestling, that is. I did get into weight lifting and lifted almost every day after school with our head football coach. I tried football in the fall but quickly got something called Achilles Tendinitis, which ended that. I gravitated back to golf. But I loved our football coach Ray Groth and years later, I would coach against him. My special team units did a good job, I must say, taking a kickoff return to the house on my Wall Right, Reverse Right return. His football team at Highland High gave up just over five points a game because they had some guy named Haloti Ngata. He would play a decade in the NFL terrorizing other teams' offenses. But I got him for six, as I like to say, and then our kickoff team had a big hit and fumble recovery inside their 10-yard line, which led to another quick touchdown. I wish I could say we won the game, but we were down 28-0 when all that happened, and we ended up losing 56-28. But Coach Groth did a lot for me, and as I got stronger and fit, my self-confidence grew. I was far from a natural athlete, and I know that must have frustrated my Dad a bit. Yet I worked hard as an athlete, but it just wasn't in the wrestling room. (By the way, Ngata took second in state in wrestling his sophomore year, but he grew too big for the 285-pound weight class and didn't wrestle after that.)

I did two camps in the summer between my junior and senior years. And it was all my idea. I found a flier in the coach's office or something about a camp held at a local high school. It might have been a two or three-day camp, and the guest clinicians were NCAA champions Barry Davis (Iowa) and Nate Carr

(Iowa State). They were fun enough, knew their stuff, of course, but at that time, college-age and still developing into adult leaders. I kept a low profile because they liked to wrestle the campers, and they didn't exactly let up or let up a lot. One camper thought he was hot stuff, and Carr really took it to him. I would like to say I gleaned some new techniques to enhance my wrestling, but I didn't. That's on me. I did, though, hyper-extend the younger brother of one of my future assistant wrestling coaches (when I was a head wrestling coach), but thankfully it was summertime, and he recovered to take second in state in a lower classification. (I wrestled 4A for the largest Utah schools back then, and he wrestled 3A.)

The second camp I went to was a fun one. I saw a brochure for a camp at North Idaho College in Coeur D'Alene, Idaho. It wasn't really the photos of the wrestling that got my attention, or any big-name clinician, but a couple of pictures of the scenery around the college. Let's just say Coeur D'Alene in the panhandle of Idaho is one of the most beautiful places on planet Earth. There are lots of pine trees and a pristine blue lake that the town is named after. In 1983, Coeur D'Alene showed signs of becoming the tourist trap it is today, but I would like to return someday and play at the golf course that has that island "floating green" in the lake. They give you two shots, if needed, to hit the green before a boat, yes a boat, takes you to putt out.

The camp was a week-long affair, and we stayed in dorms. My roommate was a wrestler from Washington. He was a 185-pounder. I thought I would be a 138-pounder, but I grew like a weed. My roommate was good-looking and well-spoken. He resembled a student body president heading to be a corporate CEO. And he was a great wrestler, too.

I had some Skyline High shorts that were gold-colored with a blue Eagle on the leg, so most campers and camp staff thought I wrestled at Skyline High School in Idaho Falls. Their school colors are similar, blue and white, whereas my Skyline is blue and gold. Their mascot is actually a Grizzly. After a while, I got sick of explaining I was from Utah, not Idaho. And many also thought I was this kid that was a state champion or something.

This kid from Montana was a state champion, or so he claimed, around my weight and was being recruited by North Idaho College, a junior college powerhouse. He was a short red-headed, well-built kid who liked to talk and talk. He was loud and popular at the camp. And I found him generally likable. As fate would have it, the camp had a takedown tournament, and we ended up in the same weight class. And when I beat him to win the tournament, it somehow made me less popular with the campers yet added to a reputation (that I was kind of tough). The immediate impact was that my self-confidence began to increase even more. And I also did fall in love with the area, so much so that three years later, I took a summer job at a Boy Scout camp adjacent to the lake not far from the town.

I know for Dakota, more is more, and he needs that experience. Unlike me, he didn't enter high school with any experience. But I had experience starting competitive wrestling at age nine and around the sport plenty before that. However, when I was Dakota's age, I was burned out, so for me, less was more. I have to credit my parents for backing off, and when I was ready to do more, I did a bit more. I refound my love for the sport. In fact, maybe I just developed a passion for wrestling for the very first time, and it took nearly until my senior year.

There were a couple of other interesting things regarding this camp. I had a (future) teammate that attended this camp. But at the time, he was a wrestler from Cokeville, Wyoming. My senior year, I walked down the hallway with my North Idaho College Wrestling Camp t-shirt on, and coming right at me was a guy, just a bit smaller than me, wearing the same t-shirt. His parents were educators, and they would always send their children to live with a relative their junior year. The reason is that they wanted their children to have access to some Advanced Placement courses that their small school couldn't provide. Remember, this was in the 1980's way before zoom meetings, or even closed-circuit TV classes, really existed. I didn't remember him from the camp, but he said he remembered me. Bryan Dayton is his name, and he was a great teammate. And now he has a doctorate. His parents knew what they were doing. Bryan qualified for state but was ruled ineligible the day before the state tournament began because proper paperwork wasn't done with his move or transfer to our school. Like his older siblings, he went back to Cokeville his senior year, placing third or fourth in state.

The other cool thing about this camp was some talk about filming this movie called "Vision Quest." Coeur D'Alene is about 30 miles away from Spokane, Washington, which was the setting for the movie. There was a lot of excitement about this movie, and some of the local high school and college wrestlers were extras. And by the way, if you read the first book in this series, you know that Terry Davis, the author of the novel in which the movie is based, wrote our last chapter. The sport of wrestling changed his life and taught lessons on how to become a good man, even if he didn't take state!

Chapter 2

DAKOTA'S HIGH SCHOOL PROGRAM SAVED FROM BEING ELIMINATED

Dan Blanchard: Wow! I can't believe it's here. It is the Monday after Thanksgiving in my son Dakota's senior year of high school. And that means that it is the first day of wrestling season for Dakota. In addition, Dan Gable just called Dakota to wish him good luck on his upcoming wrestling season. Yes. That is the same Dan Gable who went unscored upon in the Olympics and was named Athlete of the Century. Dan Gable is the Michael Jordan of wrestling. Dan Gable is huge, and that phone call was also huge!

Dakota's last chance to pursue his dream of becoming a good man through becoming a state wrestling champ is finally here. His previous two high school wrestling seasons had been stolen from him through knee surgery in 10th grade. And the pandemic terminated all wrestling in Connecticut during Dakota's 11th-grade year.

Dakota has been up against one obstacle after another over these last four years. But, in the end, adversity is what builds character, right? And that character building is what this whole wrestling journey has been all about. Everything else, like winning medals, is just gravy. We build character through doing hard things. Building Dakota into a good young man through wrestling has been our goal since we started this journey four years ago when he first entered high school.

But hey, we all know that life certainly isn't fair, and it hasn't been fair to Dakota, either. Life isn't fair to any of us. And all we can do is try to make the best of our lives and build our characters along the way. I'm sure that our Creator is more concerned about the content of our character than our creature comforts.

Thankfully, our high school wrestling team didn't fold this year. Due to Covid, several other teams around the state did fold, like East Catholic. East Catholic was my first job as a wrestling coach. Eric Gremmo and I brought it back to life back in 1990. I'm saddened to see it no longer have a program. Dealing with the pandemic and no wrestling in the State of Connecticut for the last year and a half made things tough on all of us. Also, our head coach left just weeks before the season began. But, against all odds, we found a new head coach to take over the program without any time to spare. Scot Rogers and I are still the parent volunteer assistant coaches. And we both have boys on the team. I have Dakota, a senior, and Rogers' younger son, Cole, is a sophomore. Cole has taken the place of his older brother, who graduated and went off to the Marines two years ago.

The learning curve is steep, and our new head coach is dealing with one obstacle after another. For example, because of all the competition for the gym, we now have wrestling practice from 6:00-8:00 at night. This makes it challenging for the kids who work that want to wrestle. It's also tough to get kids to come back to school after going home for the day. In addition, we also found out that our scale and first aid box are missing. And, we don't have uniforms either, nor any money in the budget to get new ones.

Sadly, we lost one of our best wrestlers, too, to a shoulder injury during football season. This really hurts our team. That boy would have been our senior captain and the main workout partner for my son Dakota. With this boy out hurt, Dakota doesn't have anyone to wrestle with in practice who can push him.

But on the positive side, it looks like we picked up two kids with experience that we weren't expecting to have. One came from the youth program the next town over in Windham, and the other is a transfer from Ledyard. Both of these new boys are looking pretty good on the mat and should have a lot of success this upcoming season.

The father-son connection between my son and me continues. Dakota entered the season weighing 154 pounds, which I, too, weighed entering my senior year. However, I went down to wrestle in the 145-pound weight class, but it looks like Dakota wants to wrestle his senior year at the 152-pound weight class, though. To tell you the truth, I think he is making a good decision because I know he will grow some more. I also know that the 152-pound weight class will be competitive. Dakota will indeed have some challenges ahead of him. But I know he's up for it. And after all, haven't the strongest and biggest trees endured the strongest winds?

The first week of wrestling is going well. Practices haven't been that tough so far. Our new head coach Bill Corrente has been very positive and passionate about building the program and building some good young men, too. Part of Coach Corrente's plan is to individually work with each wrestler to make them a better wrestler and a better person. I'm happy that the new head coach and I are on the same page to develop our young men holistically.

After being concerned that our team would fold without a head coach, we now have 17 wrestlers on our roster. About a dozen have been showing up daily, and we're trying to recruit a few more. However, some of our wrestlers work their jobs a few nights a week. And we don't have a full lineup yet. We need wrestlers for all four lower-weight classes and our two upper-weight classes. It's funny how many kids who come out for wrestling tend to land in those middle-weight classes. There never seems to be a shortage of wrestlers in the middle of our lineup.

Dakota and his teammates seem to be holding up pretty well physically to the demands of the first week of practice, which really haven't been that hard yet. Now, on the other hand, the coaches haven't been so lucky. I've noticed we coaches walk gingerly each day into and out of practice. We've also been sleeping soundly at night. It seems like the wrestling practices of the first week have been harder on the coaches than the wrestlers. Although, I did see Dakota holding his elbow that he dislocated over the summer. Later, he told me that his elbow, the bend of his arm, and even his bicep were throbbing.

Next week, the wrestling practices should get tougher for the wrestlers! The practices have to get a lot harder because we're only about 10 days away from our first match. Many of our boys are about to do the hardest thing they've ever done in their life when they step on that mat. I sure hope they don't get shell-shocked. I hope they find the strength in themselves to come back the next day to do it again.

The beginning of the second week started off really cool. Gus Dastrous, the San Francisco firefighter who started E.O. Smith's wrestling team in 1987, told me he was interested in coming to Dakota's end-of-the-season team banquet. In addition, Dakota talked to me about his senior project paper that he is doing on the benefits of wrestling. At this moment, it seems like the universe is now helping Dakota have the best possible experience as a wrestler. We tend to eventually reap benefits when we stick with whatever we're doing through the ups and downs. Wrestling is such a great sport. It's a builder of our young people, just like Dakota's senior project paper says.

However, on the flip side of that coin, the second week of the season has been very frustrating. Dakota hasn't completed a practice yet this week because of his elbow and arm pain. Every day this week, he had to leave practice early to ice his arm. I'm worried about the scrimmage coming up this Saturday at Windham High School.

In addition, two days this week, I've had to work my other jobs and had come to practice late. Coming to practice late frustrates me. And to add to my frustrations, I also tweaked my back this week at practice. Now it looks like both of us Blanchard boys are in some pain this week, and we haven't even had our first match yet.

Wednesday night, I picked up a get-well card for Sean, the boy mentioned above who should have been one of our senior wrestling captains. He was injured during football season and just had shoulder surgery. He is out for the entire wrestling season. Losing one's senior year is a very nasty pill to swallow. All the wrestlers and coaches signed the card. Then Dakota and I stopped by his house on the way home from practice to personally deliver it.

While in the car driving home, Dakota was rubbing his arm. I could tell he was frustrated. I asked him if he was okay, and while rubbing his arm, he said, "Dad, I deserve to have a chance to wrestle this year. I can't go through another injury. It's my senior year."

My heart was breaking, but I had to be strong and hope for the best. And that paid off Saturday at our scrimmage at Windham High School. Windham is a powerhouse program that has a long history of great wrestling and 10 State Championships to prove it. The Windham kids are always tough. We bumped Dakota up a weight class during the scrimmage to take on Windham's 160-pound senior captain. Dakota turned a lot of heads during that match while securing a victory with a takedown during the last 30 seconds. And to top it off, Dakota said his arm wasn't hurting too bad during that match either.

Looking back at the second week, I have felt frustrated. But, in the end, it was actually a good week. Dakota wrestled well at Windham. And our new head coach has been open-minded with his approach to wrestling. He hasn't boxed the kids in as many wrestling coaches do lately by only allowing wrestling to hit certain moves. Like myself, Coach Corrente believes that there are many ways to win a match. In addition, Corrente has given me a lot of room to jump in and show moves that complement his wrestling techniques. I like adding my expertise to the learning process for the wrestlers. And everyone benefits from it. I'm glad that our new coach is open-minded and doesn't let his ego get in the way as we all try to help our young wrestlers grow into good young adults.

Brian Preece: As I read Daniel's chapter, my mind is going a hundred miles per hour thinking about several different things.

It's sad to see programs drop. When Connecticut didn't have a wrestling season the year before, it becomes easy for administrators to cut programs. And it's especially easy to eliminate a program if they aren't competitive, lost a coach, or any other combination of factors.

In Utah, we actually added some programs from last year. Utah is a bigger state than Connecticut. Utah has a lot of land and has tons of little towns dotting the landscape. Although nearly 80 percent of the population lives along the Wasatch Front from just north of Ogden south through the Salt Lake Valley, continuing south through Utah Valley. And in many cases, the very small schools with less than 50 students will sometimes add and drop programs. They might have one wrestling mat. And if enough students (and parents) show interest, and they can find a willing coach, usually a Dad these days, then these schools will have wrestling programs. But then, a couple of years later, when interest wanes, they'll drop the program. And then the program might pop up again like a rinse-repeat cycle. Utah has about 100 wrestling programs and six classifications. The largest is called 6A and generally has schools with enrollments grades 10-12 of 1,500 or more students, though some of these schools might have close to 3,500 students. 5A is the next biggest down to 1A, where you have schools with 150 or fewer students.

Though freshmen, or ninth graders, can compete fully in high school sports, realignment is based on grades 10-12 and is done every two years. So Utah is constantly realigning. And if you kept track of the last census, you might have noticed that Utah is the fastest-growing state in our nation, growing at a clip of just over 18 percent since 2010. The Californians are moving here like droves, and our schools, especially along the Wasatch Front, are crowded with ever-changing student populations. Our state athletic association used to realign after five years. But the growth was deemed too fast, and more frequent realignments became necessary to help better ensure fair competition.

5A wrestling, not 6A, is generally accepted as the best classification in Utah for wrestling. However, there are some really tough rural programs. 5A has the most schools with 32, which means it is a bit deeper. 6A has 24 schools as a comparison. And some of the traditional powerhouses are in 5A. Most of these schools are along the Wasatch Front, with a few exceptions. One of them is Wasatch High School, which is just 30 miles east of Utah County, located in the Heber Valley, deemed the fastest growing place in the country. It is where the famous Sanderson brothers wrestled.

Then there is where my father used to coach, Vernal, which is nearly 200 miles east of the Wasatch Front. Uintah used to be a very small school, as was Wasatch. But Vernal has consistently grown with both tourism and the petroleum industry attracting people to the area. Nobody wants Uintah in their region (or league) because it is an outlier. And significant travel is required to compete against them. It's also not necessarily easy travel in the winter as going over high mountain passes is required.

Then there is Park City, just around 15 miles north of Heber Valley. This bustling ski resort town has grown rapidly over the last generation. Park City isn't much of a factor in wrestling but does have a couple of quality individuals. Then there is Tooele County, just west of the Salt Lake Valley. They have two 5A schools with solid wrestling programs but not necessarily title contenders. Uintah and Wasatch have long traditions of success. Uintah is the favorite to win the 5A, and Wasatch should be in the top three this season.

Personally, I consider Wasatch a coach's dream (in about every sport). And for wrestling, it has the nexus of small-town rural values that bring out tough wrestling kids from legacy families, along with enormous resources from a highly affluent area. The community loves its athletics and its wrestling. And the town isn't that far away from either Utah Valley or Salt Lake Valley. And that has made it an attractive place for people to relocate as you get that mountain scenery and smaller town feel with reasonably close access to big-city amenities. But I'm sure some of the longtime locals are growing tired of the growth.

I'm a bit worried about the state of wrestling in some of our urban schools. Maybe all states are like this, but Utah has a vast chasm of great programs and not-so-good programs, and not too many "middle class" programs. And the rich keep getting richer, and the struggling programs continue to struggle (even worse). And they are struggling to the point that makes me very concerned about some of these schools dropping their programs. They aren't competitive, and their numbers of participants are low.

Many urban schools have struggled with substantial demographic changes, primarily increasing Latino students. Unlike surrounding states like Arizona, California, Colorado, New Mexico, and Nevada, Utah hasn't really tapped into this Latino talent in wrestling or other sports generally, save boys soccer. And unless our urban schools from less affluent neighborhoods do a better job with this, they will struggle athletically.

The other answer is developing youth programs. The problem is that this takes long-term vision and investment. And it might not produce dividends for several years. But like anywhere else, I suppose, the strongest high school wrestling programs seem to have outstanding youth programs feeding them talent.

When I was the head coach at Provo High School (1994-2006), our program might have been that rare exception. We did compete well, producing top ten teams and state placers and champions despite not having strong youth programs. We had youth programs, but they weren't nearly as strong as most of the schools around us or certainly what my father developed at Uintah. So I just did the best I could, along with my best friend and Assistant Head Coach Darren Hirsche, to recruit in the school, focusing on football athletes and freshmen.

Football athletes are the best athletes in the school generally. And of course, with freshmen, you have the most time to develop the talent when these athletes don't have prior youth experience. We had the reputation of having good big-guy wrestlers. To me, that was a point of emphasis in our recruiting because bigger kids generally don't need to have the experience to necessarily be successful. Other programs maybe had bigger kids with youth experience. But our wrestlers were generally more athletic. And within a year or two, we could get them, to what I called "on-line", or ready to compete at the top level.

My biggest failure as a head coach was not building a strong youth (K-6) and middle school/junior high programs. But my administrators at Provo High School wanted me to coach multiple sports. I just didn't have the time to build a youth wrestling program. I coached baseball and football most years and sometimes golf when I wasn't coaching football. I also did a lot of summer baseball. So, I tried to point my high school wrestlers to off-season opportunities in freestyle clubs across the valley. But when wrestling season ended, I got a week off to catch my breath, and then baseball started. Since the city recreation programs ended in sixth grade, it then became incumbent for the high school program to also run the junior high program. One of my young assistants did both, but that was very demanding for him, and even though he ran the practices and so forth, as the head coach, I was still involved. There is only so much time and energy a high school teacher and coach has. And on top of that, I had a young family that needed my attention.

The city programs frustrated me so much that I thought about competing against them by starting my own youth program. But like I said, it's hard to do it all as a head wrestling coach. Besides that, the city was contracted to use our own wrestling room on Tuesday and Thursday nights, making pursuing this path extremely awkward. Their model of youth competition, for better or worse (and certainly worse in my opinion in training wrestlers for high school), deemphasized competition giving participants a Spartan level of competitive experiences against other clubs.

When youth wrestler parents came to me wanting an enhanced competitive experience, I would often point them to Mettle Wrestling, run by my friend Cole Kelley. When I coached, Mettle wasn't tied to any particular high school. However, you still risked having some of these athletes make friends with wrestlers who lived in other high school boundaries and did not end up at your high school. And that happened a time or two, but that's the risk you took.

The problem was I really love baseball, and it was hard to give that up and focus more on wrestling. Perhaps I was a bit cocky. I successfully took novice wrestlers who started in ninth and tenth grades and turned them into successful wrestlers, even state placers and champions. But I think youth programs have become essential as the sport becomes more and more skill-based, along with the fact that youth wrestling today can give wrestlers hundreds of matches in a year. Today, the experience gap makes it tough for novice high school wrestlers. This creates other issues in the sport I will perhaps address in a future chapter.

When I was a youth wrestler, I wrestled five or six tournaments and then state and maybe a multi-state national level tournament. Now, these wrestlers have scores of tournaments all year long. They have opportunities to be on National teams, giving them exposure to elite wrestlers all across the country and even the world. As a high school coach, you can make a heavier wrestler with limited experience into state placer/champion material. But it is rare to do that with a wrestler in the lighter and middleweights at the large-school level.

We pulled it off with a wrestler named Clay Taylor. After one year of wrestling, he placed third in state as a junior and second in state as a senior at 135 and 140 pounds, respectively. But even that was nearly 20 years ago. Clay might have been the best natural athlete of anyone I ever coached. He only had about 100 matches in his career. He didn't do fall or spring wrestling because he was busy doing other sports (competitive skateboarding) and acting. If you want a good laugh, watch the flick "Mobsters and Mormons." In it, he plays the teenage son of Mark DeCarlo's character, who is in the witness protection program and assigned to live, you guessed it, in Utah.)

Of course, I really would like Dakota to be that exception to the rule and get on top of that podium!

Chapter 3

FACING AND OVERCOMING DOUBT

Dan Blanchard: I asked Dakota on Sunday morning how his elbow and arm were doing. Sometimes things hurt more the next day. To my delight, he said his arm was still feeling pretty good. However, he complained that the knee he had surgery on was bugging him again. And his hamstring was tight again because of it. Dang! His knee and hamstring continued to bother him throughout the day. And it was painful enough for him to cancel his workout with me on Sunday night. I'm a bit worried again.

Monday and Tuesday practices were easy, which I guess is a good thing because many of our wrestlers were a bit banged up from the scrimmage on Saturday. Many of them had done pretty well in the scrimmage, but now they were paying the price for it with some minor nagging injuries.

To our pleasant surprise, a new wrestler joined our team this week. He's a senior, and he's pretty athletic. He said he wrestled in Virginia way back in 6th grade. I worked with him on Monday and Tuesday and was very impressed with how athletic he is and how fast he is catching on to the moves and being in a good wrestling position.

The new guy is an excellent addition to the team. And he's going to win a few matches for us, too. However, wrestling is always filled with ups and downs. We're trying to ride the high of doing well in Windham and the arrival of a new guy with a lot of potential. But it looks like we also lost 4 or 5 more kids this week after the Windham scrimmage. Wrestling is a very demanding sport. And it's tough to keep kids on the team when they begin learning how demanding this sport really is. Oh well, that's life. We have to take the bad with the good and then just drive on and make the best out of whatever we have.

Wow! What an opening night we had this Wednesday. We opened up our season at home against New Britain, where I teach and coached. We didn't have any wrestlers in the first four weight classes nor a heavyweight (285 lbs.) We had to forfeit the first four weight classes, but luckily, we had two wrestlers in the 220-pound weight class, so we bumped one up to the heavyweight class and didn't have to give up a forfeit there.

We started the night off with several alumni pouring into the building to watch our season opener with their parents. They got a treat. They saw a very exciting wrestling meet starting with our 132-pounder, the transfer from Ledyard.

Our first wrestler was a bit rusty out there and got caught in a few dangerous situations from a tough and talented wrestler from New Britain. But, in the end, our boy pulled out a win via a pin that fired up the crowd and got us off to a great start.

Next, our 138-pounder picked right up where he left off two years ago and was relentless with his half-nelson attacks. Just like two years ago, his half-nelsons eventually wore down his opponent, and he pinned the New Britain boy, firing up our fans some more.

Our 145-pounder received a win by forfeit from the other team. And then my son, Dakota, took the mat. Dakota looked awesome out there on the mat. He was well on his way to a technical pin in the first period when he finally pinned the boy giving us six more team points and our third pin in a row. Everyone was starting to sense that something special was happening here.

The following several weight classes, we had our less experienced kids go out there on the mat, and they all battled very hard. We lost a few matches here, but we were incredibly proud of their efforts and performance. For the last varsity match of the night, we bumped up our 220-pounder, who came to us from the Windham youth program, and he took it right to the New Britain kid pinning him in the first period. We ended the night with two JV matches, in which both of our young wrestlers really impressed us.

Our brand-new head coach, Bill Corrente, earned his first win as a new high school wrestling coach. I couldn't have been happier for Coach Corrente, our wrestlers, and all of our parents and fans in the stands. It was a great night all around and a fantastic way to start our season. We now have something to build upon. However, I've been around this sport long enough to know that there will be a lot of ups and downs coming our way, starting with this Saturday's tournament in Waterford.

Thursday morning, I woke up to a Facebook message from a wrestling coach in Maine who saw Dakota's wrestling video from the night before on Facebook. He was very impressed and wanted to talk to Dakota. This is one of those highs I was talking about up above. Unfortunately, right after that, I received a text from an Ivy League school that Dakota looked at that said their school probably wasn't the right fit. This is one of those lows I was referring to above. Many more highs and lows are still coming. It's going to be one heck of a roller coaster ride over the next several months.

Later in the morning, I saw a text from our head coach Bill Corrente telling me that he had a surprise for me that night at wrestling practice. I reminded him that I would be late to practice because I had to meet with the teacher contract negotiations team. I wondered what the surprise was. When I finally made it to practice, Coach asked me, "Are you ready for your surprise?

Next, he called some kid out of the bleachers. I then saw a huge kid stand up and begin walking toward me. I couldn't believe it. Was it really possible? This was amazing. This kid was big, solid, and nearly 300-pounds. I excitedly asked the kid, "Are you our new heavyweight?"

He responded that he wanted to learn to wrestle. I almost jumped for joy. We finally have a heavyweight. The stars are aligning for a very special kind of season, even if it still is one of the craziest seasons right in the middle of a pandemic.

"This is great, coach! You found us a heavyweight!" I blurted out to our head coach.

"You want to know what's even better?" Coach Corrente asked.

"What?" I asked.

"You're going to teach him how to wrestle!" Coach replied.

Hey, I'm more than happy to teach any kid how to wrestle. But I hope this one doesn't fall on me.

Dakota looked good and healthy going into Saturday's 15-team Lancer Tournament at Waterford High School. I couldn't say the same about myself. I gingerly walked into the place wearing my brand-new E.O. Smith coaching shirt and sporting a hyperextended knee and backache that is getting worse instead of better.

During the coaches' meeting, one of the coaches, Chris Gamble, who I used to wrestle with, came up to me and asked if he had heard correctly that there was a Blanchard in the tournament. I beamed with pride and said, "There sure is! He's 152-pounds, and he's pretty good, too!"

When I got back to the bleachers to sit with the team, I noticed Dakota's demeanor had changed some. I asked him what was going on, and he told me that he was nervous. I responded, "You're human. You're supposed to be nervous." But unfortunately, it was way beyond that for Dakota. He was so stressed out that he was making himself sick. His skin was actually turning gray, and it was worrying me.

Dakota's first match didn't help much either. He came up against a very experienced scrappy wrestler who put Dakota on his back a few times. Dakota made several mistakes that he doesn't usually make that one can't do against good wrestlers. Thankfully, Dakota pulled off a 16-8 win, but it felt like he was continuously on the verge of losing that match.

Before Dakota's next match, our head coach Bill Corrente asked me why Dakota's skin was gray. Dakota was still in his own head and couldn't seem to calm his nerves. I gave him some relaxation techniques, but it didn't make a difference. And to add salt to the wound, next Dakota faced an outstanding wrestler, who would eventually take 2nd at the State Open. This kid pinned Dakota in the first period. Everyone on the E.O. Smith's team was shocked to see Dakota get not only beat but pinned.

Things had gone from bad to worse. I knew Dakota was now psychologically bruised and would have a tough time coming back from this damaging start to the tournament. I went into the locker room and tried to soothe him and bring him mentally back into the game. I didn't have a lot of success, though.

However, our world works in mysterious ways sometimes. And I am so grateful that Dakota's old coach, Jon Torres, who just went over to coach Windham High School, walked into the room. Jon tried to console Dakota and give him some good advice when my words had fallen flat. I think Dakota needed that extra encouragement from his old coach. Thanks, Coach Torres, for putting the wrestlers ahead of wrestling.

When Dakota calmed down and was back in the bleachers, I talked with him. I told him that this was the exact moment we talked about for four years. This is when he decides if he mans-up or doesn't. This is when he gets to decide if he digs deep to come back or doesn't. He can walk into his next match telling himself how much this sucks. Or he can step onto that mat, telling himself that he owns the mat, and he will win on his mat. The choice is all his and his alone to make.

Head coach Bill Corrente also saw what was going on with Dakota, and he too pulled Dakota aside a few times for a talk. Coach Corrente knew he had to get into Dakota's head and kick out Dakota's self-sabotaging thoughts.

Maybe it was good for the team to see Dakota struggling and learn that he, too, just like them, was human and that wrestling was hard as heck for him, too, regardless of how good his teammates may think he was. The bottom line is that wrestling is brutal for everyone, no matter who you are or where you're from.

Speaking of difficulties, I'm very proud of our team. We have a very young and inexperienced team who had the odds against them, but they all fought valiantly all day long. There were so many ups and downs. And the summation of all those ups and downs exhausted our coaching staff and team. However, we landed two kids in the finals and two kids in the semifinals when it was all done. Our 220-pounder took first. Our 132-pounder, who we bumped up to 138-pounds, took 2nd. Our 152- pounder, Dakota, who bravely fought his way back, took 3rd. And our brand new 160-pounder, who we bumped up to 170-pounds, took 4th. As a team with no wrestlers in the bottom four weight classes, we took 7th out of 15 schools. That's impressive!

I am so proud of this team. These young boys were really up against a lot of adversity on this day, and they stepped up with all they had and did the best they could. Not a single kid quit on themselves or us. And that's all we coaches can ask for. This season is going to be one heck of a season, indeed!

And as for Dakota, the entire coaching staff realizes what he was up against with that gray skin. And even though the tournament didn't go the way Dakota or we had hoped for him, we also know that he had a huge mountain to climb to fight his way back for 3rd place. And he did it. And it was awe-inspiring.

When I had Dakota alone in the car for the ride home, I think we made a lot of progress on his outlook on wrestling. I think he now realizes that he doesn't have to be perfect. He doesn't have to win every match. And he doesn't have to be a state champ. He just needs to be his best version of himself. And shooting for that best version and a state championship can help him shoot for the stars and miss with the moon. If he does hit the star, he can still accomplish something amazing that he'll always be proud of. If he misses the stars and lands on the moon, he still would have been super successful and had an out-of-this-world- experience. And this moon landing, too, would lift him to an even better version of himself. And that's what we want. We want Dakota to become the best version of himself. We want him to become a good man by doing something very hard, like wrestling.

Oh yeah. One more thing. This weekend, it was awesome to see Dakota's off-season KT KIDZ wrestling teammate Ben Gorr at the wrestling tournament. Ben took second and then was sitting matside encouragement to Dakota when he was battling for 3rd place. Ben even pointed out that the table had messed up on Dakota's score, forgetting to give him back points he had earned for a Zook. Ben's mom sent me a photo of Ben and Dakota standing together, holding their trophies the next day. That picture is priceless.

Brian Preece: As I read Daniel's writing, I was thinking that I always got nervous before my matches. I always gave my opponents respect, maybe too much respect sometimes, but I didn't want to get beat. Being a coach's son, there was a lot of pressure.

Lots of people took joy in my demise, and that was just the adults.

I was always concerned about the result and not as much about the process. One of the regrets I have as a competitor is that I was so results-oriented that I always wrestled the same way. I used the moves I learned when I started wrestling around age nine and never really changed throughout college. I tried to wrestle a bit differently a couple of times. But that only lasted a few seconds in a semifinal match in one tournament, which I thought would be my last competitive match ever, my match for third place at state my senior year. I guess at that point, I said, "what the heck"? Let's try something different. But as fate would have it, that wasn't my last match, and I went back to my old ways to finish my competitive wrestling career.

It seems like the recruiting process for a possible college wrestling opportunity is out there for Dakota, and that's exciting for sure. I wasn't that recruited, but my first high school coach later became the head coach of Brigham Young University (BYU) as I was starting college. I actually got to visit BYU on an official recruiting trip. But I'm sure my experience was stranger than most.

I remember driving down to Provo from Salt Lake, a distance of roughly 40 miles, by myself. I met a BYU wrestler I knew because he wrestled in Utah at a high school near BYU in Utah County. He was a 2X state champion named Chris Humpherys. I'm not sure I made much of an impression on Chris. He showed me around a couple of buildings in the P.E./Athletics Department, where the wrestling room was. Then he drove us to the local movie theater very close to the campus, where he handed me $20. He instructed me to see "Indiana Jones and the Temple of Doom." Before he left, and I think he was bored spending time with me, he pointed in the direction of how I should walk back to the campus and to the Field House where the wrestling room was. He said Coach Albright would meet me at 4:00 p.m.

I met with Coach Albright, and that was that. No scholarship would be offered. He said if I kept my grades up and showed promise, I could maybe earn some kind of scholarship down the road. But that was good enough for me. I always wanted to go to BYU, and now I would wrestle on their team. I thought that was beyond cool. (Sadly, BYU doesn't have a wrestling program anymore as it dropped it around 1999 or 2000. I can't remember; it was just a very sad day. The only solace came when Utah Valley started a wrestling program in 2001. And some 20 years later, it had two NCAA All-Americans and two of the 20 semifinalists at the 2021 tournament. That's pretty darn cool.)

Three other schools showed light interest in me, and one was Yale. I guess my Dad had a connection there. Still, there would be no scholarship as Ivy League schools don't do those for athletics, but my wrestling would get me considered for entrance to the school. The University of Wyoming showed an interest, and so did Rick's College, now known as BYU-Idaho. Ricks College was a top-level junior college wrestling program at that time. As for Wyoming, living in Laramie, one of the most brutal places to live weather-wise in the continental 48 states, didn't sound too appealing. With Ricks College, to me, it was a junior college, and I felt I got good grades at what was then considered the top academic high school in our state. So "junior college" didn't sound that great to me. Yes, I was a bit of a snob that way back then.

I went to BYU without a scholarship. My parents and I split the cost. They probably paid a bit more than half, and I went to the financial secretary at the start of every semester and wrote a check for the full tuition. I remember the secretary thinking it was strange for me to do this. Most students going there had some sort of scholarship or pell grant or aid in some form or the other.

As a walk-on wrestler, I didn't get a lot of perks. Most of the new scholarship athletes stayed in what was called Helaman Halls. It was the dorm closest to the Field House and had the "training table" or better food. But I was in Deseret Towers, a longer walk to the athletic facilities, and not quite the menu choices. However, one of my teammates lived on the same floor as I did, a fellow walk-on. Since I was a walk-on and battling to be the second-string wrestler, I didn't take great pride in being a team member. In fact, I never mentioned it around the dorm. But my teammate took great pride and made it well known on our floor he wrestled. I felt terrible that I beat him in the wrestle-off as it crushed his spirit a bit. I think my roommate Chris Weston, who wrestled in high school but not on the team, took great pleasure in my victory as he was sick of my teammate being so boastful.

I remember being a college athlete was a bit strange. Every day before I reported to practice, I went to a cubicle in the locker room, where a pair of workout shorts and a t-shirt were placed. I didn't have an assigned locker. I had to find a locker among all the other walk-on athletes. Then after practice, I threw my shorts and t-shirt in a bin to be laundered. I can't say college wrestling was all that fun. I only missed one practice in high school because of a kidney infection (I actually went to practice and sat and watched). But since college wrestling is so brutal, quite frankly, I suffered my first injury in my back and neck. Later down the road in life, I would have a neck fusion. In college, a small fraction of athletes took some amount of joy in injuring others. After all, though we were teammates, we were still not only competing for mat time but potentially competing for scholarship money.

On top of that, the assistant coach was pretty hard on me. I explained this a bit in the first book of this book series. He saw potential in me and wanted me to give more effort, but as a 19-year-old, I didn't quite understand things like maybe I should have.

Believe it or not, the coolest thing about my first and only year of college wrestling was BYU winning the national championship in football. It was fun being inside, which means being in the locker room and weight room areas while all of that went down. And once in a while, finding myself at a party with some of the football fellas. Plus, even walk-on athletes got tickets to the football games, and our seats were really close to the action.

Hall of Fame quarterback Steve Young, who had graduated BYU the year before, hung around some. I think he was attending law school at the time. He didn't initially sign to play with the NFL but played in the USFL for the LA Express coming out of college. The USFL season was in late spring/summer versus the traditional fall/winter. So there he was hanging around the team, and since he was one of my all-time favorite athletes, I couldn't resist strumming up a conversation with him. I had to ask whether he thought he would actually get that big contract he signed. Steve Young told me it wasn't what people thought but was an annuity sort of thing paid over decades. Since the league folded, I'm not sure how much money he actually got. I won't say I was his friend or really friends of any of the BYU football players per se, but there was a fraternity of respect from one college athlete to the next. And football players knew that the wrestlers worked very hard.

As fate would have it, I would actually teach and coach some of the children of Robbie Bosco, who was the quarterback leader of this great BYU team. And I would end up coaching football at Provo High School under one of the All-Americans on that team, tight end David Mills. One of the backup offensive linemen later would become my taping partner in one of my P.E./Athletic Training courses. The guy had the hugest ankles I've ever seen. None of these people knew me as some gangly freshman wrestler, but I would later get to know them in my adult life. My taping partner Don Busenbark became a head football coach at Union High School in Roosevelt, Utah, which was the rival school to Uintah where my father had once coached. He had some success and won what I think was the school's only state championship in football. And even more incredible, his son wrestled and might have been a state champion, at least a state placer.

As far as Chris Humpherys, he would become a Western Athletic Conference (WAC) champion and wrestle in the NCAA tournament. He had two sons who were very successful wrestlers. One was a 4X state champion and All-American, and he currently wrestles for Utah Valley University.

Chris and I were about the same weight when I arrived in college. But I grew two to three inches my freshman year in college, and my weight shot straight up as well. In my fourth (and my extra fifth year of college, haha), I wrestled intramurals, where I gladly report that I won both tournaments. I wrestled 190 pounds in the first one. I expected to do the same the next year and had no idea that I would weigh in at 210 pounds and now in the Heavyweight division. I was pretty nervous wrestling guys 50 or 60 pounds heavier than I was, but I managed through okay.

I saw Dakota had grown like a weed from when he started wrestling as a freshman in the 119/126-pound classes. I can relate. When I was a freshman I wrestled 100 pounds in junior high. Then I wrestled 105 pounds as a sophomore, followed by 126 pounds as a junior. Then as a senior, I shot up to 145 pounds. Coach Albright hoped I could wrestle 150 or 158 in college, but I just kept growing. I settled around 215-220 pounds when I left college, and low and behold, in my second year of coaching high school wrestling as a teacher, here came the head coach's second son. I was the perfect size to be his main workout partner for four years. I proudly say I worked out with a 3X state champion and All-American and the first Utah wrestler to win in the Dapper Dan. I also blame Jeff (Holtry) and my ill-fated one-year foray into college wrestling for my neck fusion haha.

And for the record, I placed fourth in the Weber State Invitational, and I went 3-0-1 in my wrestle-offs. Yes, back in the olden days, they had ties. I was also one of the star students for the team, at least for the fall semester. And maybe that's the reason Coach Albring asked me to give it a try again the following year. But I would also like to think I wasn't that horrible of a wrestler...

Chapter 4

STILL WRESTLING WITH COVID-19

Dan Blanchard: Mentally, Dakota seemed to be in a better place this week. Last Saturday was hard on him. But, I asked him how he was handling it, and he said he was fine. I watched him a little bit in practice Monday night, and he looked like the old Dakota. Although, I must admit that I didn't really get that much time to watch him because I was working with our brand-new heavyweight wrestler who stands about 6'4" and weighs 295-pounds.

I am very excited about this new kid. He's full of natural talent that just needs to find a way to come out of him. He wants to eventually wrestle in college and go to Harvard Law School. Coach Corrente, Coach Rogers, and I have only one short year to help this kid reach his goals.

So, as I said above, I'm happy with the new addition to our team. Still, he has been challenging to train because he's so much bigger and stronger than me and everyone else on the team, too. He pushes me around like I'm some kind of rag doll. In addition, my backache seems to be getting worse and worse this week. And my sore back is making everything I do throughout the day more challenging. When I mentioned my back hurting to Dakota in the car ride home after practice, he reminded me of how his knee that got surgery on still hurts. That comment from Dakota pretty much put things back into perspective for me, and I stopped complaining to him about my back pain.

On Tuesday, I once again only caught glimpses of Dakota working out because I was working individually with our heavyweight wrestler again. The practice seemed to go well for all the kids. On the way home, Dakota told me that the wrestling culture and climate this year is the best that he has ever seen for E.O. Smith. I had to agree. There seems to be something special in the air about this wrestling team filled with young and unassuming boys. Most of the team is still green, but there is something special about them.

Dakota also told me that he hit a super duckunder on our 145-pounder, Ben and that Caleb, our 138-pounder, said that that was the smoothest move he had ever seen in his life. I'm pretty sure I smiled from ear to ear upon hearing how smooth Dakota looked at practice tonight, according to one of his teammates. We have to wrestle against Rocky Hill tomorrow night. And I'm hoping that Dakota wrestles well and can gain back more confidence and momentum with a good solid victory. However, only time will tell.

Wednesday was a crazy day. Dakota woke up with a stuffy nose, and I received a terrible phone call from the hospital. My father had just passed away from Covid. These two events were a lousy way for Dakota and me to start our day. However, regardless of what was going on in our lives, the team needed both of us to be at our best that night. Rocky Hill is very well-coached and would be a tough match.

We began the night by forfeiting our four lightest weight classes to Rocky Hill. Our new heavyweight also had to work, so we had to bump up one of our 220s to the 285-pound weight class, where he would have to go up against a guy a lot bigger than himself. We were at a terrible disadvantage and down by a lot of points before our first wrestler even stepped onto the mat.

But, when our first wrestler stepped onto the mat at 132-pounds, he fought hard and secured a pin with those famous half-nelsons of his. Next, our 138-pounder stepped on the mat. He quickly pinned his female opponent. Our 145-pounder, a bit green still, secured the first takedown and fired us all up even more. However, his inexperience got the best of him, and he was eventually rolled to his back and pinned.

Next, Dakota stepped on the mat at 152-pounds. Coach Rogers looked at me and said, "This guy looks good." I had to agree. The Rocky Hill wrestler confirmed what we thought by getting the match's first takedown against Dakota. My heart raced. However, Dakota stood up and got away for a 1-point escape. Then Dakota hit a beautiful high-C and took the Rocky Hill wrestler down to the mat for two more points. Okay, I thought this would be one of those back and forth battles. I knew Dakota wasn't feeling all that well... So, I was nervous. I was kind of hoping he'd have an easy match. But that wasn't meant to be, I guess.

Second period, Dakota picked down, but instead of getting back up to his feet, he got cradled and put on his back. My heart almost jumped out of my chest. Dakota bravely fought his way out of the cradle and then got back to his feet as the kid hit Dakota with a fancy trip and brought Dakota back down. Dakota immediately got back up to his feet again. When the kid tried his trip again, Dakota stepped over it and secured the reversal for two more points. Then Dakota hit the kid with a great tilt and secured three more points.

The match went into the third period, which I was hoping it wouldn't because I knew Dakota's nose was stuffed up, and he was having difficulty breathing through it. But after a flurry of moves in the third period, Dakota managed to sink in a deep half-nelson on his opponent. He drove the Rocky Hill kid to his back and secured the pin and a win for his team.

This was a great match and a great confidence builder for Dakota. This Rocky Hill wrestler was well-coached, big, and athletic. But Dakota still managed to pin him, even while not at his best. I think this is what Dakota needed. He overcame some adversity and found himself on the top. I know I wanted him to have an easy match because he wasn't feeling good. But, in the long run, growth comes best at the outer ranges of our comfort level. And this match was an excellent example of that for both Dakota and his father/coach.

Our next wrestler, who should have been wrestling at 145-pounds, was bumped up and lost in the 160-pound weight class. Next, one of our newer kids, who should have been our 160-pounder, fought a match that none of us will soon forget. At the 170-pound weight class, he showed courage beyond belief to pull off a thrilling win up a weight class. His teammates were impressed with his gutsy performance and told him so.

Next, we lost a pair of tough matches with a couple of our newer guys. When we finally got to our 220-pounder, who had taken 1st place in the previous weekend's tournament, he was fired up and ready to pound on his opponent. However, Rocky Hill didn't want to give us any team momentum, so they forfeited that weight class. We then went straight to our heavyweight class, where our very light first-year wrestler was at a big disadvantage. Our boy lost the match, and Rocky Hill secured the team victory over us. Our kids fought hard, but the inexperience combined with all the forfeits we gave up was too big of a hill to climb that night for our young boys.

Sean and his mom came out of the stands to say hi to me after the meet. Sean is the boy who was supposed to be our captain this year but injured his shoulder during football season. We sure could have used him at 170-pounds. However, it was great to see Sean and his mom. I wish they could have enjoyed a victory with us that night, but I guess it wasn't meant to be. I encouraged Sean to come on down to a practice to help the younger guys. But I could see the pain still on his face of not being able to wrestle his senior year. I doubt we'll see more of him during the season. But, I can always hope...

I had mentioned earlier that Rocky Hill was a very well-coached team. Paul Myers, who I have known for a long time, is their head coach. He is the son of Dr. Myers, who some would call a legend around these parts. Way back in the day, Dr. Myers trained our head coach, Coach Bill Corrente, whose name used to be Bill DiPietro, to multiple state titles. Dr. Myers was also my high school gym teacher. We all love Dr. Myers and miss him. There is even a wrestling tournament named after him called the Doc Myers Tournament. Well, not only is Rocky Hill technically sound and well-coached, but they are also filled with good young men and women. Without anyone asking them, as soon as the meet ended, they helped our E.O. Smith boys roll up the mats and put away the chairs. Thanks, Rocky Hill.

Right after the Rocky Hill meet, I found myself in foreign territory. Christmas is this Saturday, so we don't have any competition this upcoming weekend. Also, the school is closed on Friday, Christmas Eve, so we can't have practice on Friday. Coach Rogers suggested we give the boys Thursday off and just tell them to do some running and lifting on their own. I thought a mini-break would be perfect because Dakota wasn't feeling well. And we were still going to be able to get practices in next week on Monday, Tuesday, and Wednesday for our Thursday match. Our new head coach, Bill Corrente, saw this wisdom and agreed to give them a mini-vacation. I don't think I've ever had a little mini-vacation during wrestling season, so again, this was kind of weird, but I welcomed it. I want to give Dakota some time to get over his cold without giving it to any of his teammates.

Living in the times we live in, things just got more complicated. As I mentioned above, my father died on Wednesday from Covid. Now, it's Friday, and Dakota is still not feeling well. He has the symptoms of a cold, which are also the symptoms of Covid. Dakota hadn't been anywhere around my father, so he obviously didn't catch anything from my dad. However, he has been around a lot of other people in school and last weekend at the wrestling tournament.

Dakota is vaccinated and is scheduled to get his booster shot at the beginning of next week. So I still believe that he has just a cold that many other people also have at this time of the year.

However, we can't help but worry about Dakota, so we will get him tested for Covid just in case. I'm feeling about 99% sure he will test negative. But, if he does test positive, it's going to mess up a lot of things for him, his team, and our family. Please, Lord. Let it just be a cold...

The test came back positive. Dakota has Covid. We were supposed to be hosting Christmas at our home, but we just had to cancel it. We let the head coach Bill Corrente know about Dakota. And he let us know that another wrestler on our team also reported having Covid. This is what we were all trying to avoid. Now, what...? This is going to mess a lot of things up...

Brian Preece: Daniel's part of this chapter is heartbreaking on two levels, losing his father and now seeing his own son battle COVID-19. I can only hope for Dakota that it is a mild case, which it seems like it is the majority of the time for our younger people. I know this new Omicron variant is supposedly more contagious but isn't quite as deadly or acute as the other two variants that have hit our nation.

It's too bad COVID-19 has become political, and I tend to lose patience with people that think it's not real or not too big of a deal. Personally, I haven't lost anyone that close to me from it. But I have known some people that have lost their lives.

One of our fellow board members for the Utah Sports Hall of Fame died in October of last year. I wouldn't say we were close friends. He was a coaching legend in girls basketball in our state, and at our monthly September meeting, we ate lunch together. Less than six weeks later, he was gone.

In the last chapter, I know I also talked about my old high school and college coach Alan Albright. His own son Carl, now close to 50 years old, got COVID-19, and he was in bad shape on a ventilator, but he was one of the minority to get off it and survive. He has a long road to recovery. Another friend who is a wrestling coach got COVID-19, and he had some heart issues. He couldn't coach his team at the end of the season. He's not coaching this year; not sure if it is COVID-19 related or for other reasons, but I'm glad he got through it. My brother Scott and my sister Deanna and some of their children also got COVID-19, but it was thankfully mild in their cases.

You just never know with this virus. It seems to impact people in so many different ways. I hope it will be more like my brother's and sister's case with Dakota, and after a couple of weeks and a negative test, he'll be back competing. I know some wrestlers in Utah got COVID-19 during the wrestling season last year. After being quarantined, they were able to come back and compete. As I said, there are many unknowns with this virus, and it just hits some people harder than others. And it can strike even people considered healthy really hard.

I know Connecticut shut down high school sports last year, and Utah decided to go on with specific protocols such as regular testing for athletes. And that's where politics come in. The more liberal or progressive states are more inclined to shut down. And the more conservative states are more willing to continue on, trying to keep things more "normal." For our younger folks, to be somewhat political, I hate seeing them losing the opportunity to participate in things they love and losing the chances to compete in sports. And yet, throwing all caution to the wind, I also see as unwise. I know many in America are "done" with COVID-

19, but the virus (and its variants) doesn't seem done with us. I also tell my more conservative friends that one doesn't have to die from COVID-19 for it to significantly impact you or your family. Some long-haulers might not totally recover. Going to the emergency room or even a short hospital stay is rarely inexpensive or convenient. Yet, I am reluctant to completely shut down things, especially high school sports.

As for the vaccines, I guess I have faith in medical science. I got my original two doses and booster, as did my wife Heidi and our two children, Lizzy and Zach. I feel bad that taking vaccines has gotten political. There are a few prominent wrestling people in our state who are staunch anti-vaxxers. I cannot tell people what to do one way or the other, but I do cringe at some of the anti-vax rhetoric I see these people post on social media.

On the positive front, I am glad Dakota got a big win. I know for the growth of any wrestler, being able to win against a worthy opponent when not feeling your best is essential. Athletes will not always feel their best physically, mentally, or emotionally every time they take the mat. Still, champion wrestlers find a way to pull through in these adverse circumstances. And to me, that's what makes wrestling a great sport because it does genuinely test an individual as no other sport can, in my opinion. As that adage from the legendary Dan Gable goes, "Once you've wrestled, everything else in life is easy." I'm not sure I totally agree with this adage, if I am allowed to say that. However, I still think wrestling prepares one for life's trials better than just about anything else.

So for Dakota, I hope for a speedy and complete recovery. My heart goes out to the entire Blanchard family for losing a family member.

Chapter 5

'THIS TOO SHALL PASS' AND 'THE SUN WILL COME UP TOMORROW'

Dan Blanchard: As a wrestling coach, I've never experienced a week like this before. Sunday, the day after Christmas, I took Dakota and the rest of my family, all seven of us, to Rec Park in Windham. There, the medical professionals gave us the PCR Covid test. I was worried about the exposure we all had from Dakota. And I was praying that Dakota's first test was a false positive.

On Monday, our head coach, Bill Corrente, let me know that another wrestler on our team had Covid. Also, our athletic director had canceled our practice that day and put Covid protocols into action. All the wrestlers on our ten-person team are considered exposed to the virus. Half our team (5) are not vaccinated and thus cannot practice for the next ten days. The other five vaccinated wrestlers can come back to practice the next day.

However, two of our five vaccinated wrestlers have Covid, and a third isn't feeling well. So, those three wrestlers also have to stay home. We now only have two eligible wresters left to wrestle this week. With this in mind, head coach Bill Corrente reached out to Windham and let them know that we wouldn't be showing up for their Thursday team tournament.

Tuesday, we got both good news and bad news. The bad news was that it was confirmed that Dakota does indeed have Covid. However, the rest of our family doesn't. Because I am vaccinated and boostered, I could coach Tuesday's wrestling practice. However, when I arrived at practice, I saw only one wrestler there. The other had gone off to a high-level baseball practice that he and his family considered very important. It's a different era. With kids playing multiple sports year-round, sometimes it's difficult to tell what sports season it is. It was simpler when I was younger. Wintertime was wrestling time.

For the first time in my coaching career, the coaches outnumbered the wrestlers at the holiday practices. We've had only one wrestler to work with on Tuesday and Wednesday this week. On Thursday, the second wrestler showed up. But, on Friday, our athletic director closed the school again like he had done earlier this week on Monday. No athletes or coaches were allowed in the school building on Friday because of Covid.

As discouraging as it was to only have one and then two wrestlers to work with this week, I think we made good use of our time. We actually started off each practice warming up by playing a little basketball. Our wrestler, who came to us from the basketball team, beat Coach Corrente and me on Tuesday and Wednesday during our warm-ups. It was fun, though. After warming up, we had the luxury of rolling out only one mat section instead of all three. This made setting up the wrestling area and breaking it back down after practice easier and quicker.

By the end of each two-hour practice, I felt good about what we had accomplished with our one wrestler on Tuesday and Wednesday, and then the two wresters on Thursday. We watched the previous matches against New Britain and then Rocky Hill, and we taught both boys how they could have won each one of those matches ten different ways. By the end of our Thursday practices, I felt our wrestlers had learned a lot. I thought that our time had been well spent on these three days. I actually felt good about how we coaches had added real value to these young wrestlers' lives. We were glad to have the luxury of spending some individual time with the wrestlers. I guess this is what they call turning lemons into lemonade, right? Now I just hope they can apply what we've taught them out there on the mat in their next match.

Speaking of our next match, we don't have a wrestling meet this Saturday because it's New Year's Day. However, next Wednesday, we're going up against my alma mater, East Hartford High School. I was their wrestling captain with their present-day head coach, Todd Albert, many years ago. Todd has an outstanding team. They are big in numbers, well-coached, and tough. Some predict that East Hartford might have a chance of becoming the LL State Champs this year. And unseating Danbury's Dynasty program, which has won it most of the last two decades. We will be pairing up our ten E.O Smith wrestlers, most of whom are in quarantine right now and aren't able to work out, up against some very good East Hartford boys. I must admit, I'm a bit worried about this one. And to top it off, Dakota is still in bed sick with Covid. And if he does make it back for the East Hartford match, he will have his hands full with their 152-pounder, who is the son of my old friend Kelly Boyd. Her son

Cooper is an outstanding wrestler who had just won the Manchester Holiday Wrestling Tournament.

Covid is driving all of us crazy. The life of a wrestler is never easy. But now, throw in Covid on top of everything, and we got this thing my drill sergeants in the Army used to say a lot that I cannot repeat here because it's very inappropriate. But... I think you know what I'm getting at here, don't you? We don't like Covid... It's screwing everything up and putting our people in harm's way.

What the heck is going to happen next week when the kids all across our state bring their holiday Covid infections back into our school buildings? Right now, Connecticut is peaking at an infection rate of over 20%, our highest so far. Next week's holiday spike will probably blow us off the charts...

However, thankfully, my boss at the school I teach at just reminded me of something my grandma frequently said when I was a young man. My boss, Jay, called me today to see how I was doing with my father's death and my son's illness from Covid. He told me that these tough times would pass on that phone call. This conversation flooded my brain with the memory of my late grandma and her pearls of wisdom that I would like to share will all of you right now. My grandma frequently told me, "This too shall pass."

In closing for this week, I'd like to wish all of you a Happy New Year! And let's all pray that 2022 is the last year of this Covid pandemic. Let's hope it follows the track of the 1918-1920 Spanish Flu, which lasted three years, according to some historians. In that case, this will indeed be the last year for Covid being a series threat. And wrestling, sports, and us humans will survive this and go on to live full, normal lives again.

Rest in peace, Dad. And to all those infected, I wish you a speedy full recovery. And to all the wrestlers out there, I wish you unimpeded mat time in 2022!

Brian Preece: As we head into 2022, the Omicron variant of the Coronavirus is hitting Utah big time. This new variant seems to be a bit harder on our younger people than the previous variants, so it'll be interesting to see how things go for the rest of the season. But right now, our state athletic association is full steam ahead. Like Daniel, I'm hoping for the best, and to Dakota particularly, I wish him a speedy recovery so he can get back to his wrestling journey. When times got tough, or when my Dad saw I was down, he often had two sayings he would share. He would say, "The sun will come up tomorrow," or "It's always darkest before dawn."

There are some big tournaments the first full weekend in January in Utah. One of them is the Vernal (or Uintah) Tournament of Champions, the longest continuing invitational tournament in Utah, started by my father in 1973. A fellow Utah prep sports journalist, Kurt Johnson, contacted me a week ago or so and asked me if I knew anything about the origins of the tournament. I told him yes, and that my Dad actually started the tournament. (I'm not sure he knew my father was a wrestling coach, not sure if he knew I was a wrestling coach. I'm known more so in the Utah wrestling community these days, especially with the younger set, as a sportswriter.) After a few email exchanges, I headed to our basement storage room and went through some boxes of stuff that I kept from my father's coaching days.

It was an interesting time going down memory lane. I was seven years old when the Tournament of Champions started. I told Kurt about how I had an emergency appendectomy when I was 10 or 11, which happened the weekend of the tournament. My Mom was usually the head scorer, but she was with me at the hospital. So a tiny mistake in scoring was made, and Montrose High School out of Colorado seemingly won the tournament by a mere half-point. But then, early the next week, it was learned that Uintah had actually won the tournament by a half-point. My Mom is great with numbers, and that's why she was the Head Scorer and a pair master at so many youth tournaments over the years. So Kurt asked if he could share that story in his piece, and I said that was more than fine.

My Dad was only the head coach for five years of the tournament's existence. But the coaches that came after kept it going and, I think, expanded it in ways in which my father would be generally pleased. It's still a way tougher tournament than our state tournaments, and as it has grown in size, it's a huge feather in the cap for any wrestler who wins it. But when you have 30 plus teams, you will still have some teams that aren't that stellar. When my Dad started the tournament, it was just eight teams. All eight teams were high-caliber teams, the best from Utah and the western slope of Colorado, along with Idaho and Wyoming.

Long after my Dad left Uintah, and when I started my own teaching and coaching career, I convinced our head wrestling coach at West High School, Don Holtry, to take our team out to Vernal. We had a few wrestlers place in the first two years with our All-American Heavyweight Jeff Holtry, Don's son, winning the tournament twice. But as a team, we were in the back of the pack but improving each year.

But the third year, when we took second in the 4A state in 1994, we actually took a strong second place in this tournament. We had three individual champions and one runner-up as well. But some of our better wrestlers got beat in the semifinals. I remember my father and I weren't too keen on how the tournament was seeded, as it seemed like Uintah, the tournament host, had all the advantageous seeds. But we also fell short in some critical matches. They actually honored my Dad with a nice presentation and a nice trophy. However, I also remember my father telling me something that still haunts me. He said, "Brian, you might not get an opportunity to win a tournament like this again. Your boys need to seize that opportunity."

Though we finished second, we still had a great time. My Dad had a grand time with our team as he beamed with pride showing off all the championship banners his teams won that hung from the wall of the gym. I still vividly remember some of the other fun stuff away from wrestling on this particular trip.

We drove out in three vans, and our other assistant coach Dan Potts took some boys out near the Green River about 15 miles east of Vernal. They saw a small two-point deer that was "domesticated" by some local farmers. So it wasn't too afraid of people, and one of our wrestlers Alex Webster, tried to get the deer into the van. He was really dead set in taking this deer back to the tournament, but Dan finally talked him out of it. But the boys had fun with the deer giving it some food. They had never seen a deer so eager to be with people. Dan wanted to distract the boys a bit from their matches, trying to make them less nervous. When he arrived back just a few minutes before the round began, Don wasn't happy, but we all had a good laugh about Alex and the deer he tried to adopt. Alex was one of the goofiest and one of the best wrestlers I ever coached. I think he played up being goofy many times to make his opponents take him lightly. As an example, Alex often wore black church socks and would look as nerdy as possible as he took the mat. He would often leave his opponents painfully defeated with his wicked top wrestling skills. He placed in state twice for our program, including third his senior year.

Another vivid memory was on the drive back home to Salt Lake City from Vernal, a trip of about three hours. I was driving along Highway 40, and I noticed the van was speeding up even though I wasn't pushing down on the accelerator. I took my foot off the accelerator altogether, but the van was still gaining speed. I was then starting to panic and about to hit the brakes hard, then I noticed one of the wrestlers was lying on the floor and was pushing the accelerator. Then, all the wrestlers in the van busted out in laughter. I told them I wasn't amused, but I admit they got my gord pretty good. I believe it was one of the Haaga brothers (Brandon or Aaron). They were definitely lighthearted practical jokers, but they could bring it on the mat. Brandon, the oldest brother, took second in state, while Aaron placed third.

Each of the coaches had a group of wrestlers who generally traveled with them. We had a truly diverse team and a diverse coaching staff, and how the wrestlers grouped up on our road trips generally showed this.

Our head coach had some of the more serious and straight-laced guys on the team in his van, as you might expect an older head coach to have. Besides his son, our other state champion Brandon Dansie, not to get mixed up with the lighter-hearted

Brandon Haaga, would ride with him mostly. But sometimes Brandon would ride with Dan or me, and if our vans got separated from the pack, often because Dan liked to make a detour or something, Brandon wouldn't like it at all. He was one of those wrestlers that liked being at the weigh-in with plenty of time to spare, and he was convinced we wouldn't make it on time. And I think Dan enjoyed poking him a bit, as did some of his teammates. I think Dan's goal was to get him to relax a bit, but I'm not sure that it worked. Also, I'm not sure it was all that needed because Brandon ended up being a 2X state champion, undefeated his last two years of high school wrestling.

My bunch generally lived in the "avenues" of downtown Salt Lake City, the affluent area that fed into the school. And they were generally the practical jokers on the team, who just had a lot of fun in life. They were risk-takers, and some of their adventures skateboarding, or even sledding, made me cringe wondering how they were still alive. Maybe they were drawn to me because I was the younger coach who played the music they liked. Sometimes, I was just the target of a lot of their pranks as the naive young assistant coach who was quick to forgive. But I know if push came to shove, they respected me as I did them. One of these wrestlers, Jason Finlinson, assisted me for a few years when I became the head coach at Provo High School. His oldest son Jacob, who graduated this past year, was a 4X finalist and 3X state champion in 6A, our state's classification for the largest schools. His sophomore daughter Emmy took state last year in our first official girls' state tourney. I joke with Jason, along with Jacob and Emmy, that I'm their "Grandpa Coach."

If kids loved the outdoors, especially hunting and fishing, they would likely travel with Dan. He had plenty of stories to share about his adventures. I call Dan the last of the hunter-gatherers out there, at least in America. His wife Karen is the breadwinner, but Dan contributes mightily to their household, as he is truly a voracious outdoorsman. He brings something home about every time he hunts or fishes. He also spends a lot of time gathering wild mushrooms and asparagus, along with a litany of wild berries. Their backyard is short on sod but big on growing everything under the sun, from berries to squash to tomatoes to corn to what I call the Simon and Garfunkel spices. Karen is a great cook, and I love their big-game dinners with plenty of great side dishes from their garden. Dan has a Master's Degree in Ichthyology, which means he's a fish expert. He was also a Peace Corps volunteer in Ecuador. So let's just say he has led an interesting life that would capture the interest of many high school wrestlers, and me, for that matter.

I think about these fun times I had coaching, these trips where I could get to know these young men away from the mat, and it brings me back to the present. Amid the COVID-19 pandemic, one can't take anything for granted. This is hard for Dakota and Daniel, and the entire Blanchard family. As I reflect on the challenges we face with the pandemic, I think of how my 1993-94 team at West High School was diverse but close and unified in the spirit to be the best at wrestling they could be. And they were just fun humans to be around. I would love for Dakota to have his own set of fun and joyful experiences as he heads into the final half of his senior year.

Chapter 6

BAD WEATHER AND COVID-19 REARING THEIR UGLY HEADS IN CONNECTICUT

Dan Blanchard: Here we go. Week six! It's Monday, and we have 8 of our 10 wrestlers back for practice. For 90% of them, this is their first wrestling practice in 10 days. The boys looked like they were moving in slow motion today. The wrestlers were slow at everything they did, from putting out the mat, warming up, drilling, wrestling, cleaning up, and even putting the mat away at the end of practice. I found myself frequently clapping my hands and hooting and hollering to try to get them to move faster, but nothing seemed to work. Maybe they had too many holiday cookies still sitting in their guts...

Fresh off of a Covid infection, Dakota also looked tired today. We're not ready for our Wednesday match against East Hartford, ranked #10 in the state and quickly moving up. But, it seems like East Hartford might not be prepared for us either. The other day, their head coach, my old buddy Todd Albert, told me they were down to only five kids practicing because of Covid. It was the perfect storm. Both of our teams were decimated with

Covid over the holidays. Most of our wrestlers just got back. And now there is a new record-breaking Covid rate of 24% in Connecticut. So, we decided to postpone our wrestling meet against East Hartford to later in the season. I guess the much-anticipated match that Kelly Boyd and I have been talking about between our sons will have to be put on hold for later in the season.

I feel a little better knowing that we now have a few more days to get the kids back in the groove of wrestling again because they didn't look much better at Tuesday's practice. I found myself yelling out a few times that it seems like they haven't sweated off their holiday cookies yet. Once again, the wrestlers looked lethargic and nowhere close to being in wrestling shape.

On a positive note, I was happy to attend practice on Tuesday due to the wonderful gift of Zoom. I am a teacher and coach and a teacher union officer. So, Tuesday, I had two union meetings to attend, one for the city I teach in, and the other was a state-level meeting. Before Covid hit our country, I would have had to be in person at both of those meetings and would have missed wrestling practice that day.

However, thanks to Zoom, I did my first meeting in my car on my hour's drive home. Then I did my second meeting while eating dinner, driving Dakota to wrestling practice, and as the wrestlers were rolled out the wrestling mats and warmed up. My zoom meeting ended just before the coaches took the mat. Now's that's some pretty good multitasking and good use of time, wouldn't you agree? Thanks, Zoom.

I was also happy that I spent some time individually going over the wrestling videos with some of our wrestlers of their previous matches with them this week. I saw the light go on a few times in my wrestlers' eyes when I explained little things to them that they could have done differently. Then I had them practice these new moves with me so I was sure they could execute them next time. A few of them even said, "Man, if I had known that before, I would have won that match." My response was, "Well, now you do know it. So, the next time you meet up with that kid, you have a much better chance of beating him."

A crazy ice storm rolled in on Wednesday morning, right during the morning commute. This made my hour-drive to work very dangerous. There were car accidents and bus accidents all over the place. Educators everywhere were complaining about how terrible the drive in was and upset that school superintendents put staff, students, and families in danger by not delaying the start of school.

Later that morning, I received a text message from the E.O. Smith athletic director saying, "All practices, events, and games today are canceled." I guess our wrestling meet with East Hartford was destined not to happen on its scheduled night. Now, I don't feel so bad that we pulled out of the wrestling meet with them earlier this week.

We let our wrestlers know that they needed to get some kind of workout in on their own and to lay off the leftover holiday cookies that night. We're missing another opportunity to get a wrestling practice in that we had scheduled in lieu of the meet. And that's not a good thing, considering how much the boys have already missed and how none of them look like they're in wrestling shape. In addition, they all have a bunch of holiday weight to lose, too.

Thursday was a tough day in many ways. Our head coach Bill Corrente decided to pull our team out of Saturday's tournament in Lebanon. He was concerned with our wrestlers' safety and didn't want to repeat the earlier Waterford Tournament. After the Waterford Tournament, Waterford's team was shut down because of Covid. Two of our guys caught Covid at that tournament, and 90% of our team had to go into a 10-day quarantine. Just getting back from that fiasco, Coach didn't want to immediately go through the same thing all over again.

Furthermore, Covid has been spiking in Connecticut since the kids returned to school from vacation and brought their unknown Covid infections back into the state's school buildings. In addition, we did an internet search that revealed that very rural Lebanon has had 80 new Covid cases in just the last two weeks.

These are unprecedented times for us wrestling coaches. And our new head coach was stuck between a rock and a hard place here. He knew pulling the team out of the Lebanon Tournament would create a firestorm. Still, he thought the wrestlers' safety and their families' safety was more important, and he'd have to take the heat. A firestorm did erupt. Our team is 50% vaccinated. So, some of our wrestlers, our families, and some of our coaches agreed with Coach Corrente. The other half of wrestlers, families, and coaches thoroughly disagreed and thought Coach was making a mistake, and they loudly let him know it.

Once again, I just wish this Covid crap would just go away... Wrestling is hard enough without all this other crap from Covid. We don't need the constant starting and stopping of our season. We don't want all the politics and strong emotions whirling around in these uncertain times.

However, carry on, we must, even if we're limping through it all. Only seven wrestlers showed up for practice on Thursday night, and one of those had to leave early to go to work. There wasn't much energy in the room that night. And on top of it, we all received messages that a big snowstorm was rolling in early the following day, and school and practice would be canceled for Friday. We just can't seem to get into a groove this season. We have way too many days off. And our numbers are meager, making it tough to get in good workouts. And we have discord over Covid and how many safety precautions to take.

Furthermore, Dakota's knee has been hurting him all week, and his thumb injury just won't heal. I've been taping his thumb before practice every day for the last month. And I have yet to see the spark and the love of wrestling in Dakota's eyes this week. He looks like he is physically and psychologically struggling with all that is going on. And to top it all off, I still can't get him to listen to me when I tell him he has to loudly project his voice as the team captain and have some authority in his voice when he's leading his team in warm-ups... There is no get-up-and-go in his voice, just like there hasn't been any get-up-and-go in the team's performance lately.

This has been a real lackluster week. And now, instead of wrestling this weekend, it's time for me to grab my shovel and begin my multi-day task of shoveling my 465-foot dirt driveway out from underneath more than a foot of snow. Good old New England... Maybe, we'll get a whole week of wrestling next week.

Brian Preece: The first full weekend to the second full weekend in January is probably the apex of Utah wrestling. Teams couldn't compete or even practice, on Saturday, January 1. But the second Saturday was the second day of many prestigious tournaments like the Tournament of Champions in Vernal, Utah–the tournament started by my Dad. And the Richardson Memorial, hosted by Box Elder High School. Some of our state's best wrestlers went to the Doc Buchanan tournament hosted by Clovis High School in the Fresno, California area. At this point, this tournament might be the toughest tournament west of the Mississippi, surpassing even the Reno Tournament of Champions. Our state had four wrestlers place in the tournament and Pleasant Grove, who has won 10 of the last 11 largest school championships, placed 19th out of 105 schools that sent wrestlers.

Then on Tuesday, we had our All-Star Dual. The All-Star Dual is where each classification has a team of its best wrestlers (at least at the midpoint of the season). There are six boys and four girls teams, and we even have some junior high matches. The event ran a little long this year, in my humble opinion having more girls matches than in previous years. (I have suggested that the boys and girls have their own separate events next year.) But this is a big event to raise money for the only college program in our state right now, Utah Valley University. And it's a lot of fun to see a 3-time 1A state champ mix it up with, say, a returning 6A state champion.

Then on the following Saturday, there was the Rockwell Rumble. The tournament attracted 68 teams this year. But the number of participants was down from its peak in 2020 before the pandemic. My friend Cole Kelley started this tournament and had to find a different location for the fourth straight year. By 2023, he hopes to have a permanent home for this event at the indoor facility for our professional soccer team, Real Salt Lake.

COVID-19 has impacted the tournament. Last year he had to do it Sunday-Monday of the Martin Luther King Jr. holiday weekend. Because Sunday participation is not particularly supported by the Church of Jesus Christ of Latter-day Saints or the Mormon Church, Utah participants were way down. But this year, there was way less out-of-state participation because the Omicron variant has caused states to limit out-of-state traveling. For example, several Las Vegas teams pulled out last minute because Clark County School District shut down its schools for five days and placed a moratorium on all athletic competitions. There were a lot of top Utah wrestlers missing as well, many out with COVID-19 and some injured. The tournament was still very high quality, with most of the brackets around 40-50 wrestlers, but down a bit over past pre-COVID-19 years.

Some of these prestigious tournaments have come under scrutiny because they have had girls wrestling tournaments associated with them. But many of the girls (and some of their parents and coaches) feel that they have been treated unfairly by being relegated to the auxiliary gyms and not given the nicer awards that were given to their male counterparts. So I'm waiting for this to hit the papers (or the media) if it hasn't already. This year, Cole has publicly apologized and promised the top placers in the Girls Rumble the nice Rockwell watches he has given to the top three boy wrestlers over the years. I was very pleased with his proactive approach.

While the Rockwell Rumble was going on, I was down announcing at the Beehive Brawl. The Beehive Brawl is a very large youth tournament in the central part of the state. This year, it attracted wrestlers from California, Colorado, Idaho, Nevada, New Mexico, Wyoming, and, of course, its host state, Utah. We had just over 1000 wrestlers and maybe around 75 girl wrestlers. But we made sure the girls that placed and won the tournament got the same exact stuff the boys got. I don't want to say that this should be obvious, but I think some mistakes have been made, and a lot of learning is going on. Girls' wrestling is still sort of a new frontier. And I think we need to show some amount of patience and understanding, or whatever one might call it when mistakes are made. I mean, look how the NCAA treated women's basketball players compared to the men this last NCAA tournament, and the NCAA has had women's basketball for decades.

I know the level of girls wrestling is not anything near the boys, nor is the participation generally. Still, when it comes to awards and recognition, equity is important. But beyond medals, other issues must be hammered out in our state. Such as; facility usage, schools finding girls coaches, and not just saying the boys coaches should just do it. Also, we have to find a way to deal with the reality that many schools have only one or two girls. We have to do more to promote the sport and help these girls from small programs gain better access to practice partners and competitions. The problem is, in many cases, if programs have only one or two girls, they are stuck practicing with the boys. And then either find competitions on their own or go with the boys where they are traveling and hope they can find some matches.

Overall, girls wrestling is exploding in our state as some programs have dozens of girls on their team. One school even has over 50. But a good portion of girl wrestlers come from programs where there might be just one or two girls on the team. Billy Cox, a leading advocate for girls wrestling in our state and a coach of a top program himself, has a motto, "All girls deserve a team!" So he has allowed girls from all over the state to come practice with his teams. And he makes sure every girl at a competition has a coach in their corner.

So this is what's been going down in Utah; while it seems in Connecticut, things are going a bit slow with canceled tournaments and meets. A few high schools have gone entirely online, but it's still full steam ahead as far as sports are concerned. Individual wrestlers might miss a meet here or there, but nothing has been canceled on a broader level. And it's not like Omicron is not hitting Utah. In fact, the Beehive State made national news by having the fourth highest case rate in the country.

Utah starts and ends wrestling before Connecticut, so we are just basically a month out before our last state tournaments are done. Our divisional or state qualifying meets are just two weekends away, basically. So I'm glad that Dakota has a bit more time to get better and get back to practicing with his whole team. Time is on his side. And I agree with Daniel; I can't wait for COVID-19 to go away. Let's hope Omicron is the last "variant," and some amount of normalcy can return to our lives!

Chapter 7

A TIME TO REFLECT ON THE GOOD THINGS WRESTLING BRINGS

Dan Blanchard: This season doesn't seem to be getting any easier or closer to normalization. I found out over the weekend that two more of our wrestlers have Covid. My heart goes out to them and their families. In regards to wrestling, thankfully, no one on the team is considered a close contact, so we don't have to send most of our team home again for another ten days. However, Dakota and the other boy who previously had Covid don't seem 100% back yet. There have been some glossy-eyed looks and complaints about being tired and not feeling well from both wrestlers. And since I live with Dakota, I can see what he is saying is true.

Early this week, we had some good news and bad news. Our female wrestler returned after being away for almost a month. We were happy to have her back but then found out that we only have her back for Monday night practices and Wednesday night matches because she's working. Hmm... this doesn't feel normal at all.

In addition, our new head coach, Bill Corrente, showed up on Monday with size-15 wrestling shoes that he bought with his own money for our heavyweight wrestler who hasn't competed yet. We're really excited about our heavyweight. He's over six feet and close to 300 pounds. We know he's going to win some matches. He's very big and very strong, as well as very smart, too. Sadly, though, the wrestling shoes sat unused this week at wrestling practice because our heavyweight didn't show up. We finally tracked him down after a few days, and he told us he quit because wrestling was interfering with his job and school grades.

The shoes showing up without a wrestler to wear them feel like déjà vu all over again. Earlier in the season, one of our custodians spent his own money to buy our triplets wrestling shoes. He wanted those three boys to have a chance to succeed in life by building some self-discipline and success through wrestling. And then the triplets made some bad choices and had to leave the team. That was another heartbreaking one. What a waste... Those three brothers had so much potential, just like our heavyweight does. However, as any coach will attest, it's not easy to keep wrestlers. An unlimited number of things can pull wrestlers away from the team. It's so hard to keep kids with potential in this sport, especially when you tell them that they're going to have to take some lumps now to be rewarded later. Even buying them wrestling shoes doesn't always work in keeping a kid on the team.

However, in contrast, we had a great Wednesday night this week! RHAM came to our school to wrestle us. My old East Hartford buddy, Ryan Fitch, runs the RHAM program, and he's had a lot of success over the years there. Sadly, we began the meet by giving RHAM five forfeits because we didn't have any wrestlers in those five weight classes. Giving another team five forfeits means we were down 30-0 before the competition began. However, that insurmountable hill of being down 30 points didn't seem to affect our E.O. Smith boys at all. They went out there and started the meet with a bang by pinning their first four RHAM opponents. Our wrestlers that followed equally stepped up to the task, and all wrestled great matches. In the end, we lost 42-36. I told the kids that I didn't care what the score said. In my eyes, they were winners that night.

I said the same thing that night to my son, Dakota, too, as he took the mat against RHAM's Class M State Champ. I told him that I didn't care what the score was at the end. I just wanted him to wrestle courageously. Knowing that he's still not 100% back from his previous Covid infection and that he wasn't in wrestling shape yet, beating a Class M State Champ was a pretty big ask.

But, just like the rest of the team, Dakota did not disappoint. He did indeed wrestle courageously. Dakota got the first takedown of the match and thoroughly controlled his opponent in the first period with a score of 6-2. Although he didn't do as well in the second period, Dakota was able to get himself out of trouble and still had the lead. Going into the last 30 seconds of the third period, Dakota was still up by one point, 8-7, when the RHAM kid, who was on the bottom, started coming up on him. All Dakota had to do was have patience and hit the Navy move at the right moment. Dakota would have brought the kid back down to the mat and rode him out for the win. Sadly, Dakota's mind was foggy, he was having trouble breathing, and he had next to nothing left in the gas tank. Dakota hit the wrong move, resulting in him being reversed and the other wrestler taking the lead for the first time in the match 9-8. Then the RHAM kid immediately put a chicken wing on Dakota and turned him to his back. He held Dakota until time expired, winning 12-8.

Dakota lost in terms of points, just like our team had lost to RHAM. But, I couldn't have been prouder of Dakota and his team. Everyone stepped up and wrestled their hearts out during these crazy Covid times that have repeatedly interrupted our workouts. It was indeed a courageous and honorable performance by all of our E.O. Smith boys. And that is the character of good young men. Like we're in right now, wrestling and adversity in times of uncertainty force our young boys and girls to step up, mature some, and become good young men and women.

The rest of the week continued to be rough. Midweek, I slipped on ice in our school parking lot and took a nasty fall, messing up my knee and reinjuring my totally replaced hip. I couldn't wrestle with the boys and had a hard time showing moves in the second half of this week. But, just like my old wrestling days, I refused to give up and worked through the pain. The six boys who showed up at practice on Thursday and Friday needed their coaches' full attention and help.

Dakota, too, was in rough shape the second half of the week. He got his Covid booster shot on Thursday and was miserable in practice Thursday night and even worse on Friday night. In addition, Dakota was still five pounds overweight on Friday night and had swollen lymph nodes in his armpits and neck. He also had a rash on his face from the booster shot. Furthermore, he couldn't lift his arm anymore and kept closing his eyes in what looked like a micro-nap in between activities. Head Coach, Bill

Corrente, told me that I should probably keep Dakota home from Saturday's tournament. He wanted Dakota to sleep and get well so we could have him back for next Wednesday's match against Enfield. I agreed with him and kept Dakota home the next day.

We only brought seven wrestlers to the Griswold Tournament on Saturday. I was calling them our Lucky 7 because, during these times, I knew we were lucky to have them out there on the mat, and I just knew they were going to have a good day.

While our Lucky 7, most of whom were still very green wrestlers, were battling out on the mats, I talked to other teams to find out if they had any openings on schedule for the next two weeks. All of our opponents have canceled their meets with us for the next two weeks due to Covid. It's crazy, but we have no one on our schedule right now to wrestle for the next two weeks. Fortunately, I found a couple of teams to wrestle over the next two weeks who have also had teams back out on them due to Covid.

Our mostly green Lucky 7 did awesome at the Griswold Tournament. Without their team Captain, Dakota, our Lucky 7 took on a lot of full teams and still managed to place 7th in a 14-team tournament. One of our 220-pound wrestlers, who we bumped up to heavyweight, took 1st place. Our 132-pounder, who dropped down to the 126-pound weight class, took 2nd place. Our 138-pounder dropped down to the 132-pound weight class, took 3rd place. And our brand new first-year wrestler at 220-pounds took 4th place. It was a fantastic day for all of our wrestlers. All of them wrestled great matches against high seeded wrestlers. For example, our still green 138-pounder pinned his first guy, then he took on the #1 seeded wrestler and took him into the 3rd period before losing to him by pin. Next, he took on the #2 wrestler in his weight class and gave him a great battle before losing. We couldn't have been prouder of our 138-pounder even though he didn't place. This was probably his best day of wrestling so far. And that's something he should be proud of, regardless of what the score said.

After all, wrestling is just the vehicle we're using to develop promising young men and women. Our wrestlers don't have to always win to have won. If they are facing their fears, doing hard things, and giving it their all, then they have indeed succeeded in my eyes and hopefully have won in their own eyes as well.

Brian Preece: Reading about Daniel's week actually made me think of a wonderful recent memory. I, like many coaches, put our scant stipend we get for coaching back into our programs and into wrestlers. Whether it be buying wrestling shoes or for someone's overnight trip, coaches give back all the time.

Many of my colleagues, former students and athletes, their parents, and my own family gathered to congratulate me on finishing my teaching career at my retirement reception. When I got back home, I had a card from one of my wrestlers that I coached around 15 years ago. Inside the card was $150 and a message that brought tears to my eyes. He basically thanked me for being his coach. And he somehow knew that I paid for his trip when we went out to the Reno Tournament of Champions. I asked the wrestlers that wanted to go for $150 for travel, food, and lodging. At first, he told me he couldn't go because his family couldn't afford it, but I told him we had him covered. I wanted him to go and have this competitive experience against some of the best wrestlers in the country. I didn't ask or expect to be paid back. It's just what coaches do. It's what my Dad did for many of his wrestlers.

For some reason, I couldn't let his nice gesture go unrequited, so I messaged him on Facebook. I had to tell him thanks for telling me thanks. I told him what he did truly touched my heart, and I would take some of the money and take my wife out on a well-deserved dinner date as a small payback for her sacrifices. But then the rest of it I would put into the scholarship fund I set up to honor my best friend Darren Hirsche, who had just passed away ten months before I would retire. If you haven't read the previous two books in the series, which I hope you do, Darren was my longtime assistant wrestling coach. He contracted a devastating genetically passed terminal disease called Huntington's disease. It forced Darren to leave teaching early at age 50, and he would pass away six weeks before his 53rd birthday. So for the past few years, we have given a scholarship in his honor to a deserving student-athlete at Provo High School.

Another memorable moment was when one of my former wrestlers did a Facebook Live with me to thank me. Sean D'Haenens is flying the big jets, and one of my deepest regrets in coaching was when he lost in the heartbreak round just before placing in the top six at state. I apologized for being outcoached in this match, and he told me it was all good. And it's all good. He's doing his dream job and has a beautiful family. He and his older brother Matt wrestled for me while I coached his younger brother Chad in baseball. His Dad is still involved in the sport as he prints off these incredible brackets our state association gives to the state champions. Matt has even officiated. It felt so good to know that I made a positive difference not just for these young men but for a family. That family has given back to the sport decades after competitive days were long over.

My retirement reception was truly a highlight of my career in so many ways. I felt so touched and humbled by all the people who came. It was truly touching to me, whether it be the more recent students and athletes or the ones from decades ago. In many cases, it was the parents that really got under my skin in a good way. Just the thought of them coming back one more time to thank me and our program for making a critical difference in their son's life gives me goosebumps. I have to admit that I was afraid no one would show up at my retirement. I didn't really want to do this reception thing, typically done for retiring teachers. Like most teachers, I made a display of sorts with old photographs and some of the awards where I had been recognized and our teams' trophies. Since I had focused only on teaching the last few years of my educator career, some of the newer administrators were shocked that I was an accomplished coach.

Another touching thing I remember about that night was my friend Andy Unsicker driving up from a small town called Richfield, some two hours. Andy didn't have a son wrestle for our program, and when I first met him, he was a vendor. He became our program's most reliable vendor for equipment and medals/trophies for tournaments we hosted. Andy just loved wrestling, and we became quick friends. He then started this big youth tournament called the Beehive Brawl, which we hosted one year at Provo High School. Years later, it is now in a big college arena in Richfield, and my role went from doing Track Wrestling for it to just being the announcer. But him making it up to Provo to wish me well in my next chapter in life really meant a lot to me.

I missed my friend Darren and felt bad he never got the send-off he deserved. He was an incredible educator, a top-rate teacher, and a coach beloved by so many. He was a much better teacher and coach than I ever was. He deserved so much better. And when I looked over and saw my Mom, it made me miss my Dad wishing that he could have been there, too.

I had a dream, or nightmare, the other night where Darren and my father had starring roles. I say nightmare because the context (or plot, if you could call it that) was not pleasant. In real life, my father basically died suddenly. He had a stroke but never regained consciousness and died ten days later. He died not much older than I am right now. With Darren, his death for me was actually more painful. I got to see him wither away from Huntington's disease, a shell of the man I remembered coaching alongside me in wrestling and football. So while the context of this dream was not pleasant, when I did wake up in a sweat, I actually couldn't help but smile. In this dream, I got to hear the voices of my father and closest friend. I saw my friend Darren smile for the first time in years, and my Dad was yelling at me, as he often did, to drive better. I guess Driver Education teachers can still haunt you long after their gone in one's dreams.

Chapter 8

GREAT WRESTLING COACHES MAY PASS AWAY BUT THEIR LEGEND NEVER DIES

Dan Blanchard: Dang! Just found out that our wrestler who took first place over last weekend's wrestling tournament caught Covid there and is now out for the next ten days. Two other wrestlers are considered close contacts, so now they are out too until at least the end of the week. This is so frustrating. We've been to two tournaments so far, and in both tournaments, we've had kids catch Covid.

However, somehow in the middle of all this craziness, over the last several weeks, Dakota and I have sort of created a new ritual or maybe some normalization during these uncertain times. Here is the pre-practice routine that has slowly developed for Dakota and me. We leave our home at 5:15. Get to the high school at 5:30 for our 6:00 PM wrestling practice. Dakota and I are usually the first ones there. My security badge gets us through the front door. However, the gym doors are typically locked. So, I often find a way to sneak in the back through a locker room or find a custodian to open the front gym doors.

Then Dakota and I move the mats out of the storage room and into the back gym. There we roll the mats out as other wrestlers slowly trickle in.

After the mats are in place, taped, and washed, Dakota and I head over to the first aid box. I then tape his thumb to give him some relief and support from the tendinitis pain running down his thumb to his wrist. Unfortunately, his thumb is just one of the many injuries he is nursing right now.

Wrestling really has a way to beat one up and humble one with the pain it causes every single wrestler, and most coaches, too.

In the early part of this week, Dakota and I had an awkward moment when we disagreed on a move I was teaching the team. I was teaching the technique my way when Dakota got up and offered his input showing another way. Although Dakota's approach was good, I spoke too hastily over him and told the kids to do it my way. Then seeing the pain on Dakota's face, I tried to correct myself and said, "If my way doesn't work for you, then try Dakota's way." Regardless, I could tell that I hurt Dakota's feelings and made him feel less than when I cut him off and told the kids to do it my way.

I could have had more tact in delivering my message and instruction to the team, but being human, I didn't. I screwed up that communication between me, Dakota, and the team. I wish I had approached that moment in a different and better way. I asked Dakota to show his way again, but the damage was already done, and he said, "No. It's okay. We'll do it your way."

Later, Dakota pulled me aside and insisted on showing me what he was trying to teach the team. He explained to me why his way was a good way. After listening to him for a while, I agreed that his newer way made sense and that he had mentioned a few things that I hadn't really considered. I guess I just automatically defaulted to what I had grown up with and what had worked for me. I think this moment was enough for Dakota, and he didn't seem like he was mad or hurt anymore. Thank goodness.

The last thing I want to do is make any kid feel bad about speaking up and sharing something that they think will help their team. And I especially don't want to discount my son. I'm glad we're both back on good ground. And as the adult in the room, I'm going to have to do better next time and make sure that I'm being a life-long learner and not just falling back on my old ways. I have to give Dakota a lot of credit for pulling me aside later and advocating for himself and what he was trying to teach the team. I'm impressed. And this is precisely what we've been trying to teach him through the sport of wrestling.

And now that Dakota's back in the right state of mind, let's hope he can deal with all his little nagging injuries and have a good night wrestling against Enfield High School this Wednesday.

Speaking of Wednesday, I barely made the team bus because of work and the hour drive to get home. But thankfully, I did make it. When I boarded the bus with Dakota just as it was getting ready to leave, I counted only six wrestlers, including Dakota. Once again, there has been nothing normal about this season.

After a good hour on the bus, we arrived at Enfield High School and saw that they had about 15 wrestlers ready to go.

They, too, were having some issues with Covid. As I talked to their head coach, Coach Flynn, I received a little jab in the ribs and turned around to see Enfield's assistant coach Paul Diaz. It was great seeing Paul again. We played together on the same East Hartford High School State Championship football team in the 1987-1988 school year. And Paul was also our heavyweight wrestler and my teammate on our wrestling team back in the day. When I saw Paul, I smiled ear to ear as we did our best to catch up on what we've been up to in just a few minutes. Head coach, Bill Corrente, laughed and said, "Gee, you seem to know someone everywhere we go."

Regardless of the low numbers we brought, we had a good night. Coach Flynn, who I used to watch wrestle for Enfield during my early days as a coach, was a beast back then, and his present-day team was built in his image. He told me he had a bunch of young scrappers, and he wasn't kidding. I told him that our teams are similar in that respect. We are a young team, too, filled with a bunch of scrappers who will fight to the end. And that's what happened. Both teams fought every match hard until the final whistle, and it was a great night of wrestling.

In regards to Dakota, I became slightly nervous when his opponent came out. The Enfield kid looked like a wrestler. This could be a tough match for Dakota, I thought. However, Dakota got the first takedown and seemed to set the match's tempo. Later in the first period, he put his opponent in a double chicken wing and put him on his back with it. Once again, Coach Flynn was correct. His kids were scrappers and fighters. The Enfield kid was upside down in a double chicken wing for a while but refused to be pinned. And he eventually even fought his way out of Dakota's pinning combination and came back to his stomach.

"Wow!" said Coach Corrente. "I've never seen a kid not get pinned when he was caught in a double chicken wing. That's a tough kid."

"True, indeed!" I said, agreeing with Corrente.

Dakota had a real fighter on his hands. But, Dakota had also taken a commanding 5-0 lead. And shortly into the second period, Dakota extended his commanding lead to 10-0. Then Dakota put the Enfield boy on his back again in the third period. But once again, the boy refused to be pinned and fought his way out of the pinning combination. However, at this point, Dakota's lead was too great at 17-1, and the referee stopped the match and gave Dakota the win by technical fall, which gave us five team points.

It seemed like Dakota's match of no one giving up was indicative of the entire night. Both teams fought really hard and refused to give in to their opponent. Our coaching staff and Enfield's coaching staff were both very proud of our young wrestlers. They made up for what they lacked in experience with effort and heart. And it was a fun night of wrestling to watch for everyone. And even though we had no chance of winning that night because of all the forfeits we had to give up. When the end of the night came, we had actually won five matches and lost two. In our eyes, we saw that as a good night of wrestling for our E. O. Smith boys.

On the way home on the bus from Enfield, I discussed with the head coach, Bill Corrente, that Covid is running wild through our high school. We had 76 cases this week. I suggested that I call Gus Dastrous, the founder of our E.O. Smith wrestling program, who is now a San Francisco fireman. I thought we should tell him that he probably shouldn't come to our end-of-the-season wrestling banquet. This decision was breaking my heart. Gus is an old friend and teammate, and I really wanted to see him and hang out with him. And he has such an amazing story on how he began the E.O. Smith wrestling program. I thought our wrestlers could only benefit from hearing it and meeting the legend who made it possible for them to have a team. But, I didn't want to put Gus in harm's way. Coach Corrente agreed with me. And I made the call to Gus.

The craziness continued throughout this week. As I had mentioned before, the team that we were supposed to wrestle this Saturday canceled on us because of Covid. Well, luckily, we were able to schedule Coventry High School to wrestle with this Saturday, instead, But now that one has just fallen through as well. Neither one of us can get our buildings for Saturday. We now, once again, have no one to wrestle on this Saturday. So once again, we'll have a Saturday practice instead of a Saturday wrestling meet.

And during these end-of-the-week practices, which included another day off because of snow, I somehow hurt my upper right thigh. It hurts to even walk on it, let alone show the wrestlers technique. I mention this new pain on top of the knee pain I'm still having from falling on the ice last week to Dakota on the ride home. As he's pulling the tape off his thumb, he says, "Dad, I can't remember the last time my knee and Achilles didn't hurt, along with a bunch of other stuff." Once again, Dakota put me in my place. Man's oldest sport is often Man's most painful sport too. But, hey, that's what this is all about, huh? We're building good young men and, these days, good young women too by doing hard things like wrestling, chasing wins, dealing with never-ending adversity, and dreaming of a state championship.

Brian Preece: Congrats to Dakota on his big win, and it seems like he's rounding into good form going into the late stages of his senior season. As a Dad and coach, this is what you hope for.

It was an eventful week in Utah wrestling. Perhaps the most beloved figure in Utah wrestling passed away–Darold Henry. Coach Henry incidentally was my Dad's biggest rival at Uintah High School. Both were young coaches at the time. When Coach Henry passed away, he was 78 years old. My Dad would be 81 if he was alive.

In 1972 both my Dad and Coach Henry won state championships at Uintah and Pleasant Grove. It was my Dad's fourth state title in a row and second for Coach Henry. Uintah won the classification for the smaller "B" schools, and Pleasant Grove won the "A" classification. But for the 1972-73 season, our state athletic association decided to create four classifications, with 4A being for the largest schools and 1A for the smallest schools. It so happened that Uintah and Pleasant Grove were put into the new 3A classification. So I imagine Utah wrestling fans were wondering what would happen when the two returning state championship programs were put together.

Well, Uintah, and my Dad, won the first 3A state title. Incidentally, my high school counselor at Skyline, Perry Gillette, was the head coach of Granger High School when they won the very first 4A state title. Then in 1974, Pleasant Grove won the state title, and Uintah placed third, which was the lowest finish my

Dad had in his 12 years as the head coach of the Uintah program. Then from 1975-1977, Uintah returned to the top of the classification, and Pleasant Grove was second twice and third once during those years. The 1976-77 season was my Dad's last at Uintah High School. For the 1977-78 season, my Dad coached Cyprus, a 3A school in the Salt Lake Valley.

An interesting twist of fate happened when Darold Henry's brother Chuck became the next Uintah head coach. And Uintah would win the next three 3A titles from 1978-to 1980. So in 13 years, Uintah had won 12 state titles, nine with my father and three with Chuck Henry at the helm.

My Dad's relationship with the Henry brothers was complicated. There was love, but there was also rivalry. But oftentimes, competing wrestling coaches can be good friends. My Dad really was fond of Chuck and was glad he was his successor. But then their relationship somewhat soured in the immediate years after Chuck's hire. I think even Darold's and Chuck's relationship had some bumps during this time as Pleasant Grove finished second, third, and ninth from 1978-80 when Chuck's Uintah teams were winning titles. I won't assign blame but only say that successful coaches have large egos. But over time, offenses were forgiven, and wounds were healed.

My Dad coached at Cyprus for four years, and though he improved the program, Cyprus was never a threat to win the state title. Then Uintah's streak of championships ended in 1980. In 1980 Uintah won the state team title without a single individual state champion. I think that's only happened twice in our state's history. It suggested that Uintah's total dominance of 3A wrestling might be threatened. In 1981, Uintah slipped to third and then placed fifth in 1982, the lowest finish for Uintah in 20 seasons. I'm not sure about the details of Chuck's departure as the head coach, though just in his mid-thirties, he would never be a head high school coach again in Utah. The very successful junior high coach, Leon Smuin, took Uintah over in 1983, but just for a year. Then one of my Dad's former All-American wrestlers, Ed Johnson, was the head coach for the next few years. Smuin won the state title in 1983, and Johnson won another three state titles before retiring from coaching after the 1988-89 season.

Being the successor to my Dad and Darold had to be hard. Both Chuck, and Tom Phelon (who took over for Henry at Pleasant Grove), had to feel the pressure of extremely high expectations from communities that expected championships. Any coach succeeding a very successful coach has to wrestle with both high expectations and to put their own imprint on a program as its leader. It's not easy. Just ask the coaches that took over after, say Dan Gable at Iowa or college basketball's greatest coach, John Wooden, at UCLA.

As for Darold Henry, he kept coaching at Pleasant Grove, leading the program for 25 seasons. The Vikings didn't win a state title from 1975-to 1985, but in 1986 Pleasant Grove was back on top and then won another title in 1989. Before retiring, Darold Henry would win three more state titles from 1991-to 93. He would come out of retirement in 1997-98 to lead Lone Peak High School, a brand new school that split the Pleasant Grove and American Fork student bodies. He also became the school's athletic director. My sister Deanna was hired there to be the volleyball coach, winning five state titles as fate would have it.

When my sister won her first state title, at the assembly to celebrate the team's success, she asked Darold to speak in which he did a wonderful job.

Darold's legacy is really too immense to describe in part of one chapter of this book. It would require a large book, which I might take on someday. His coaching tree is enormous. He coached Steve Sanderson, the father of Cael Sanderson, who is now leading Penn State. Steve actually coached ten state title teams himself. Three of our valley programs are currently led by wrestlers he coached in high school or youth programs. He has two other former wrestlers leading programs in California and Idaho. One of his former wrestlers was a successful head coach and now is a head principal in Cache Valley in northern Utah.

Darold Henry also taught driver education, was also a head golf coach, and helped out with the football and track and field programs. Beyond that, he was a significant church leader in the community and a volunteer firefighter. There is hardly a soul in Pleasant Grove that wasn't touched by this man. And I need to mention he was one of the best officials in the nation and officiated in 31 NCAA Division I championships. He was the lead official when Pat Smith won his fourth NCAA title.

I went to Darold's viewing (or wake), where you can give your respects to the family members. I arrived 15 minutes early as I anticipated a large crowd. However, I didn't anticipate well enough because a long line of people had already gathered. I have never in my life seen a viewing with so many people. His death was sudden and not expected. He appeared in good health recently in public at the Uintah Tournament of Champions and at a Pleasant Grove basketball game where his grandson Payton was honored for reaching the major leagues for the Miami Marlins. He had a heart attack while walking his dogs. His last words thankfully were in the presence of his loving wife of 56 years, Bell.

Besides being great wrestling coaches, my Dad and Darold had another thing in common in what they said to me. My Dad's last words to me were, "I love you." It's why I try to say that to my children every night where I can, either in person or through text. The last time I saw Darold was at a Mexican restaurant at the mouth of Provo Canyon. Our meeting was sheer accidental though Darold was evidently a regular at the place. I was just driving back home from Heber City, and my wife Heidi wasn't home, so I needed to get my own dinner. I always wanted to try this place, and I was thrilled I did. Darold invited me to his table, where we swapped stories about my father and wrestling. As we parted ways, he said, "I love you, Bri." That meant a lot to me then, as it does now.

Earlier in the week before Darold's passing, I got a phone call from my friend Leanard Garcia. Leanard was an assistant coach for my Dad at Skyline High. Like how I broke into the coaching ranks, he was a student-intern coach who ended up staying on at Skyline for Dad's entire tenure there. Leanard did have a connection to my father, as he wrestled for Joe Wolfe Davis, who wrestled for my Dad at Uintah. Davis was a senior on my Dad's first team as head coach and technically the third state champion my Dad ever coached. Davis became a very successful coach, winning seven state titles at Monticello High School in rural southeastern Utah.

Leanard earned the nickname FUBAR (yes, it's an acronym that many would know, especially if you served in the military) from Coach Davis. But this time, it was a term of endearment, and FUBAR was written on the plastic sweats he often wore to practice. So that became his nickname for us Skyline wrestlers as well. As it turned out, he was the longest-serving assistant coach ever for my Dad. And when my own relationship with my Dad struggled, he was there for me as a listening and supporting ear.

Leanard, by the way, has enjoyed reading the first two books of this series, *Hitting the Mat* and *Trying to Take the Mat*. I'm embarrassed, though, that it's taken me until this third book to mention him by name. He was a vital part of that village that helped me succeed as a wrestler and coach. And since Leanard was much closer to my age than my father, we developed a good friendship now going on nearly 40 years. Leanard didn't go into teaching or coaching but worked as a firefighter for the U.S. Forest Service, rising up the ranks to a lead supervisor before finally retiring about the same time I did. He is a great man and deserves special mention as one who served my father faithfully, and he remains a dear friend to me and the rest of our family.

Coach Henry's death and Leanard's phone call caused me to think deeply about the sport of wrestling and the profession of coaching. A great coach has enormous impacts that are generational. My father and his rival took different paths. My Dad left Uintah at the peak of his success at age 36, while Darold stayed at Pleasant Grove and became an icon to that community. A small handful of coaches have truly shaped Utah wrestling, in which they are both a part. I would like to believe there is a heaven, and both of them are swapping stories and laughing, no longer rivals but just friends once again enjoying wrestling.

Chapter 9

BEING THERE AFTER A TOUGH LOSS

Dan Blanchard: So, here we are going into the last full week of January. I'm beginning to feel like the end of the wrestling season is coming too fast. We only have a few weeks left, and then our regular season will be over. The Class M State Championships take place on the third weekend of February. That weekend will be the end of most of our wrestlers' season. A few who place in the tournament will get a chance to go to the State Open Championship the following weekend. And then, that will be the last weekend for most, if not all, of our wrestlers who made it that far. If any of our wrestlers place in the State Open Championship, they'll get one more week of wrestling. Then their season will end on the first weekend in March with the New England Championships.

I feel a little sad knowing my time as my son's high school wrestling coach is coming to an end soon. These four years have gone by very fast. I can still remember when the last day of his senior season seemed so far away. I'm so grateful for having the opportunity that so few fathers get. And that opportunity is being their son's high school coach. But, with the sweetness of this privilege also comes the bittersweetness of thinking it will be over soon. I know all this will soon be in the rearview mirror as just a memory of the many ups and downs that we shared together.

This week started off pretty normal. At least one kid was missing because of Covid. And at least one more kid was missing each day because of work obligations. Eight kids showed up on both Monday night and Tuesday night for practice. Coach Corrente is hoping that next year he can change our practice times from 6:00-8:00 PM to when school lets out at 2:30. I hope he is successful because 2:30 would be a much better time for our wrestlers and a much better time for Coach Corrente too, now that he works at E.O. Smith High School.

In the same vein above, I even told a kid on Tuesday night that we should be able to double our numbers next year. And that he'll most likely have someone next year to wrestle with that is the same size as him.

Injuries continue to plague our wrestlers and some of our coaching staff. Several of our wrestlers are walking around with bruised ribs. And Coach Corrente is just getting over his sore ribs. Dakota has nagging injuries all over his body. Lately, his Achilles tendon has been flaring up to the point where it feels like it's burning. I'm a little worried about Dakota right now. And I'm still dealing with my own injuries as well. My hip is better, and my knee is almost better from that fall I took last week on the ice. But, my right upper thigh is still hurting and making it so I can't do much on the mat. Coach Rogers thinks my thigh problem was probably from that same fall in the school parking lot last week.

However, regardless of how much we all hurt. Wrestling must go on. So, it does. And we all grind our teeth and persevere. And while we continued to grind it out, Coach Corrente approached me on Tuesday with an opportunity to relax and do something else for a couple of hours. He had an extra UCONN vs. Georgetown basketball ticket for that night after practice. We're both UCONN alumni, so he thought I might like to go. I did indeed want to go. We had a good time watching UCONN blow out Georgetown and their coach Patrick Ewing in our old stomping grounds, the UCONN Gampel Pavilion. All those UCONN National Championship banners hanging up by the rafters looked awesome up there. We had a good time at the game, but I don't think either of us liked it much the next morning when our alarm clocks went off so early for another busy day.

Wednesday's wrestling competition was canceled. The meet was another victim of Covid. And it looks like a massive snowstorm is moving into the state for Saturday too, which will no doubt cancel that competition as well. As I drove Dakota to our Wednesday practice, instead of a meet, he looked despondent. I asked him what was going on, and he told me that his whole body hurt. He said that he has injuries everywhere, and there's nothing anyone can do about it. I'm very worried about Dakota. It's breaking my heart to see him like this.

While walking into the high school for wrestling practice, I saw our 132-pounder walking down the street toward the high school. He had just gotten off the city bus. I'm so proud of this boy. Every night he takes the city bus so he can go to practice. He does what needs to be done to get to practice. It's impressive. And every night of practice and every match he wrestles, he does nothing less than give 100%. He's such an amazing young man. He's someone you can always count on.

Now in another vein, our 138-pounder missed practice on Wednesday because he was trying to help out a stray dog that afternoon, and the dog bit him in the face. This wrestler is such a kind and wonderful boy. He has undoubtedly been raised right. But regardless of his love for living things, stray dogs included, we sent a message to him through his team's group chat to stay away from stray dogs from now on. Hopefully, he'll listen. But... probably not. I imagine his big heart will get the best of him again someday in the future.

Wednesday's practice started off at a snail's pace. The boys are getting lackadaisical. They're getting slower and slower at doing what they need to do to the point where it seemed like laziness to me. So, I called all the wrestlers to the center of the mat and had a little talk with them. I needed to remind them what good young men are all about. I needed to remind them that good young men don't take the easy way out and don't let laziness get the best of them. I might have even gone a little overboard. I told them that wrestling wasn't anything compared to what still lay in front of them regarding the challenges of being a good man. I told them the challenge of being a good man in the work world, someday as a husband, and even eventually as a father would be more challenging than wrestling for them. But, it was something they would have to step up to and be a real man about. And that doing precisely that in wrestling gave them a springboard and advantage to the tough times they will face as an adult.

Coach Corrente commented that I was getting a little heavy with them and that they were still struggling just to get a girl-friend. He was probably right. But, I still think that our wrestlers needed to hear what I had to say. They need to step up in prac-tice these last few weeks. And I also told them that I didn't care if they place in States or not. But, if wrestling helped them be better young men who were better prepared to take on the world after wrestling, then our coaching staff had done everything it was supposed to do. I sure hope this big picture thinking didn't go way over their heads. I hope my little speech got at least a few of them thinking about seizing the moment and working hard toward becoming good men. Their teammates are counting on them, as well as their future family and this country.

About halfway through the practice, Dakota approached me and told me that both of his arms were killing him. I looked at his arms. And both hands were once again shaking as if someone had just slammed them in a car door. I don't know what is going on with Dakota. He has been in agony much of this season. I'm wondering if he might have caught Lyme disease in the past without us knowing it, and now it's resurfacing and wreaking havoc on him. I don't know what else to think right now. I don't seem to have any answers to what is causing him all this pain. I can see on his face that wrestling isn't fun for him right now. And with this being Dakota's senior season, this is the last thing any of us what for him as he is finishing up his wrestling high school career.

Our Saturday meet was salvaged thanks to our athletic direc-tor, Dan Uriano. Dan is friends with the Manchester High School Coach and athletic director. After some problem-solving, he rescheduled our Saturday match to Friday night in some small back gym at Manchester High School. It will begin at 4:00 PM to hopefully help us get in the meet and get out of there before the big weekend snowstorm arrives.

When I arrived in Manchester, I saw an old colleague of mine was the referee. Scott Inman was the referee for our meet. Scott used to coach Maloney High School's wrestling team way back when I coached New Britain. It was good to see him again. I noticed he was moving gingerly. When I inquired what had happened, he told me he fell on ice that morning and hurt himself. Hurt or not, he knew he had a job to do. The wrestling meet must go on, no matter how painful it was. Boy, everyone involved in wrestling is a warrior, from the wrestler to the coaches, the referees, and even the parents who go the extra mile every day.

Well, it worked, and we got the meet with Manchester in before it snowed. And once again, we gave up a bunch of forfeits and didn't have much of a chance of winning the meet. In addition, Manchester came out with a very athletic team and really gave us a hard time. Manchester's athletic boys quickly pinned our green wrestlers and gave our more experienced ones a tough time. Many of our boys wrestled bravely, and I'm very proud of them whether they won or lost.

Dakota's match was once again very indicative of the night's wrestling. A very athletic Manchester boy stepped on the mat against Dakota. Dakota wrestled the boy well and got in on some very deep shots that the Manchester wrestler physically worked his way out of. Then Dakota hit some misdirection stuff, and the Manchester boy looked like he was in trouble but then, through his athleticism, worked his way out of that situation too. The match was still 0-0 going into the later part of the first period when Dakota finally got a takedown after much effort. The Manchester kid was so athletic that he got up and out of it, and Dakota couldn't do anything about it. The score was 2-1. Eventually, Dakota hit what looked like some kind of trip/throw that landed the Manchester boy right on his back, but the fall had taken place out of bounds, so it didn't count. The first period ended with Dakota ahead 2-1. Dakota had controlled almost all the action in the first period. He appeared to be the better wrestler and in control of the match but was only up 2-1 going into the second period.

For the second period, the Manchester boy picked down. Dakota set up on top, and wrestling began. Dakota was doing a great job breaking the other kid down and riding him. Dakota kept trying to secure an arm, but the athletic Manchester boy wasn't letting him get it. And every time Dakota took his weight off him to attempt to secure his opponent's arm better, the boy was back up in his base and moving away. During one of these exchanges, the Manchester wrestler exploded to his feet, and Dakota got caught a second behind him, still on his knees. One cannot wrestle a very athletic kid from their knees, even if it's only for a second or two. The Manchester boy, from his feet, used his athleticism to Head Chancery Dakota to his hip. Dakota got back to his belly, but the damage was done. No one on their belly was going to have a chance against such an athletic kid on his feet. The Manchester Wrestler drove Dakota to his side and then his back. Then he squeezed the heck out of Dakota and pinned him.

It was so frustrating. We all knew Dakota was better than his opponent. Coach Rogers turned and looked at me with sadness on his face and said, "That sucks. Dakota lost that match because he made just one tiny mistake."

"Yup," was all I could say, as my facial expression answered Coach Rogers back.

After the meet, while I explained to Dakota what to do next time in that situation, we both received a pleasant surprise. Arfan tapped both of us on the shoulders and said hello. After exchanging huge hugs, we tried to catch up some. The last time we saw Arfan was over the summer at Shirzad's house when Arfan was training to compete in the World Championships. He had worked out with Dakota a bunch of times over the previous summer. He was always offering Dakota advice on what to do to improve in wrestling. And this encounter with him again, right after the Manchester match, was no different. Arfan was jovial and congratulated Dakota on the good things he did out there. Then he offered some advice on what to do next time to avoid losing to this kid again.

It was awesome seeing Arfan again. He offered us an open invitation to train with him again anytime we wanted. This is one of the beauties of this sport of wrestling. When one wrestles, they meet people from all over the world who are high-quality people and very friendly and helpful. There is a real brotherhood in wrestling. Wrestlers, no matter where they come from, are like family. The wrestling community is filled with good young selfless men, and now these days, good young women too.

Now it's time for me once again to put down my pen and pick up my shovel. Our area of Connecticut is getting 24 inches of snow. I sure hope we don't lose our electricity. And since there obviously won't be any wrestling on Saturday, we told the wrestlers that their Saturday practice is to shovel their driveways. And then go help a neighbor do the same. It's our duty as wrestling coaches to continuously plant the seeds of what it means to be a good young man and even a good neighbor too.

Now for a quick side note. My alma mater, East Hartford High School, coached by my old buddy and teammate Todd Albert, has just been ranked #5 in the state and looks like they will continue to climb. Way to go, Todd and the East Hartford wrestlers! You East Hartford wrestlers are now chasing the title of Best East Hartford Wrestling Team Ever. You're attempting to knock the 1987 team where Todd Albert and I wrestled side by side and back to back in the State Championship Finals off the throne. Good luck.

Brian Preece: After reading Daniel's section, my head is buzzing about many things. I think good and certainly great coaches see that participating in sports is more than just wins and losses. It's about creating quality young men and women.

Like most coaches, my assistant coach Darren Hirsche and I would gather our wrestlers at the end of practice. As sweat dripped down their faces, we always seemed to impart some closing thoughts of wisdom like Daniel. We always made a point to thank them for being there and their efforts in practice. We might have had some other team business to remind them of. But then we talked a lot about the importance of academics and being good citizens. These things were important to us. And not just to Coach Hirsche and myself, but to all the coaches on our staff.

As for me as a wrestler, I don't have too many deep thoughts about my last high school match. And in fact, what I thought was my last high school match wasn't even my last high school match. I was literally a last-minute replacement for a wrestler at a postseason all-star dual event. I went there to watch and ended up wrestling. And as fate would have it, I would win that match. I still would have rather taken state, but it helped lessen the immediate pain of not reaching that goal. To be honest, I don't dwell (at least very little) about my fourth-place finish at state. In fact, as time passes, I'm more proud of what I accomplished versus being disappointed. I did better than most, and I'm satisfied with that.

I think my not taking state led me to my teaching and coaching path. It gave me more empathy and understanding. Most wrestlers (and athletes in any sport) will end their careers with a loss. It is the slim minority that gets to go out on top, say like John Elway, with a win in the Super Bowl. At our state meets, 14 wrestlers will be state champions, and the rest will have some level of disappointment. So it is essential to think beyond winning and losing as the ultimate measure of success, especially in youth and high school sports. The journey, in my mind, is more important than the destination because the journey (of life) doesn't end with the state wrestling meet.

I know I take the losses of my athletes very hard. So hard that years later, I actually find myself apologizing to them for not being a better coach. And it's the truth. I know in many instances I got outcoached. But being the great men they turned out to be, they instead often comfort me and praise my efforts in coaching them. They remind me of the bigger picture.

It does seem in some sense, and I don't want to cause trouble here, that losses in team sports like baseball and football are sometimes harder on kids and coaches. But then again, maybe not. But I have been in some really tearful locker rooms or team meetings after losses in the state playoffs in baseball and football.

I was an assistant baseball coach for many years. And we had two excruciating losses where in the semifinals (the top three in the way our state baseball tournaments are run), we were literally one out and even one strike away from advancing to the state championship game. But we couldn't get that last out, much like the Boston Red Sox in Game 6 of the 1986 World Series. Then the team that beat us went on to take state, which made it even more painful.

In football, it might be harder because the number of games one gets to play is way less. And then that final loss in a season of 10 or 11 games really hits hard. One such memory that stirs me is when we lost in the playoffs in what I thought was my last season as an assistant football coach. We had this African-American player that joined our team. He had a tough life and him becoming academically eligible was quite the feat. But he wanted to play football, and to me, this is another testament to the importance of extracurricular activities like sports in helping to keep at-risk kids in school. But as the team, including the coaches, had tears in our eyes at the end of the season, I made eye contact with this young man. And then all I could do was hold him in my arms as he sobbed, and then we wept together. I had those fears for him that football was the only thing that kept him connected to the school and a more productive life path. As it turned out, I was both right and wrong. He had some rough patches, but he is rebounding, trying to build a better life for himself. I would like to think football and caring adults (his coaches) made a difference.

In a previous chapter, I described how I shared tears with wrestlers in the arena's tunnel at the state meet. Their seasons come to a close with heartbreak. This is where I think you earn your keep as a coach. But another burning memory is of a loss that didn't happen at a state meet but at the qualifying region meet. This wrestler made it to the blood round, the round before placing in state as a junior. In his quarterfinal match, he even threw the returning state champion Cyler Sanderson, the younger brother of Penn State head coach Cael Sanderson, on his back. We didn't pin him and lost by major decision. But it's a great memory for both of us.

This young man had a solid senior season and placed third at the Rockwell Rumble (or whatever it was back then), which is our state's toughest tournament. But at the region meet, he got upset in the first round of the tournament. He was seeded third. The second seed also got upset, and then he was put out by that wrestler in the next round. There would be no state tournament. Our school was hosting the region tournament, and I told my assistant coaches they would need to take care of things for a few minutes. I needed to be with this wrestler. His Mom was one of my favorite parents and actually worked as an aide at the school. Mom and I were trying desperately to console him, and yes, there were tears from all of us.

Braeden Woodger was one of the best team leaders we ever had. I often joke that he was my all-time favorite wrestler to coach, not that he was the best wrestler but a great team leader who always thought about the team first. And he was a "thrower and goer," as my Dad would say, and had a really fun style of wrestling. I needed him to know that I was proud of him and felt his pain. He deserved better, but this was what life handed him. But he took that lemon and made lemonade, and he gives back to the sport to this very day doing Track Wrestling at many wrestling tournaments across our state.

For many years, I took him with me to help run events, but he became the real master, and he is the one that most often gets called now. And when I find myself running an event, he's always there to help. He coached a little bit at the high school, but this is how he gives back, helping to run events so others can have quality competitive experiences. His own boy is now in youth wrestling. He also just finished the basement of our new house, and at our former home, he built our deck and a really cool shed. He does great work and gives me the "family rate," which I am more than grateful for.

As a competitor and coach, you seem to remember the losses better than the wins. Maybe if you take state or nationals, it is different. And coaching a state championship in youth baseball was a lot of fun. But those losses on the diamond, or gridiron, or the wrestling mat are often the ones still haunting me in my dreams. Even my father, with all of his successes, still rues the few losses he took. He never seemed to grow tired of telling the story of how one of his wrestlers, Eugene Woody. Eugene tried to be the first Native American in our state to win three state titles. He was screwed out of winning that third state title by the referee, thus denying him All-American status. I'm pretty sure Eugene dealt better with the loss than my Dad seemed to. But when you love your athletes, you want them to have success. You want them to be champions. But as the title of our books suggests, if one can't take state, it's essential to be a good man.

Braeden Woodger and Eugene Woody are good men today, and I'm sure, win or lose, Dakota is on the right path to do the same.

Chapter 10

LEARNING LIFE LESSONS FROM LOSSES ON THE MAT

Dan Blanchard: Well, this week has started off a little different. We began the week with a wrestling match against Putnam High School on Monday night. And although, as usual, we had one of our best wrestlers out for Covid, and another out because of work, it still felt very different to wrestle competitively on a Monday night. Our meets are always on Wednesdays and Saturdays.

Unfortunately, we forfeited six weight classes. Putnam High School was already up 36-0 before our first wrestler stepped onto the mat. However, when we finally got the chance to put our wrestlers on the mat, they did not disappoint. Our 126-pounder, our 132, and our 138 started us off with three straight wins. We lost 145. But then got back on a roll again when Dakota pinned his opponent in the first period at the 152-pound weight class. Then our 160, 182, and 195 pounders followed up with great victories of their own. It was a great night of wrestling for us. We won seven out of our eight varsity matches, equaling an

88%-win ratio. We began the night down by 36 points and came roaring back to losing only by only two points. It was a pretty good night of wrestling for us.

On the way home from Monday night's wrestling meet, Coach Corrente gave me his coaching key. He's headed out to a family wedding in Washington D.C. Coach Rogers and I will run practice for a few days and do the Wednesday night Bristol Central meet without our head coach this week. Thankfully, we're more than able to do it.

Sadly, our school budget doesn't include an assistant coach for the sport of wrestling. I feel that is wrong. And I hope Coach Corrente doesn't have to rely on volunteers like Coach Rogers and me in the future. Hopefully, someday, Coach Corrente will have a paid assistant coach who he can count on to help him out with the program after Coach Rogers and I are gone. Coaching a high school wrestling team is just too much work, with too many moving parts for just one person to proficiently do. If Coach Rogers and I weren't volunteering our time, Coach Corrente probably would have had to miss a family wedding. And I don't think that's right. He needs a paid assistant coach.

Tuesday's practice went well. I finally taught our kids some leg wrestling. And Coach Rogers and I did our best to get them ready for the very competitive Bristol Central team we would be wrestling on Wednesday night.

I'm a bit nervous about Wednesday night to tell you the truth. Bristol has a large successful youth wrestling program that makes their high school wrestlers tough. In comparison, most of our high school wrestlers have way less experience than the Bristol kids. And that puts us at a significant disadvantage.

In addition, Dakota's opponent is an outstanding wrestler who just beat the Platt boy who will eventually be the Class M State Champ later in this season. Once again, Dakota will have his hands full with his opponent, and he's going to have to be at his best to beat this kid. But I know he can do it.

We arrived at Bristol Central Wednesday night after an hour bus ride. It was nice to see an old colleague of mine still around, the Bristol Central head coach, Archibald. He was coaching Bristol Central way back when I coached New Britain in the late 90s and early 2000s. I recognized referee Matt too. Dakota and I saw Matt refereeing in Spooky Nook, Pennsylvania; Dakota wrestled in a wrestling tournament there over the fall. I'm still amazed and delighted at how small the wrestling world is and how often I see someone I know in it.

Unfortunately, we were down four wrestlers against Bristol Central. We were already behind 24-0 before our first wrestler even stepped on the mat. I knew every one of our wrestlers had a tough match ahead of them. And those tough matches started with Dakota this time. The 152-pound weight class went first, and Dakota took the mat against their senior captain hammer.

I was pleased with Dakota's patience in the first period. He didn't rush his moves. Dakota wrestled the first period smart and even hit a beautiful arm throw that I thought would put him up 5-0. But that didn't work out when the Bristol captain immediately spun out of the throw once he hit the mat. The first period ended 0-0. Dakota controlled the tempo and wasn't in any trouble of being scored upon in the first period.

In the second period, Bristol chose down. Once again, Dakota wrestled smart and did what he needed to do. The Bristol wrestler was tough, but Dakota held him down and kept the Bristol kid's weight on his own hands or on his belly. Dakota wasn't successful in turning his opponent, but he did the next best thing. He rode his opponent hard and wore him out some. It was a dominating performance in the respect that the Bristol kid, who is used to having his own way, couldn't get out from the bottom. And so far, he hadn't even come close to scoring a single point on Dakota.

The score was still 0-0 going into the third period, and Dakota picked down. Dakota reversed his opponent about twenty seconds in and went up 2-0. Since Dakota successfully kept the Bristol boy down in the second period, I imagined Dakota doing it again in the third period and winning the match 2-0 against this talented Bristol wrestler. With about 40 seconds left, Bristol escaped making the match 2-1. We all knew that a takedown was going to win the competition.

With about 20 seconds left, the Bristol kid got in deep on Dakota's legs, and Dakota was a split second too slow in reacting. Dakota went down to his hip and then butt. He tried to fight out of it, but in time, the Bristol boy finally secured the takedown and went ahead 3-2. Dakota immediately got up to his feet and tried to get away. The Bristol boy held on for life, and the time finally elapsed. The Bristol boy was declared the winner, 3-2.

It was a great match, and I was so proud of how hard and how well Dakota wrestled. I know Dakota wasn't happy with the loss. But I didn't mind the loss so much. I was proud of Dakota's effort to do something challenging and then be a gracious loser when things didn't work out the way he had hoped. In my eyes,

Dakota had an outstanding performance. It appeared that Dakota was the better wrestler, even though this Bristol boy had just beaten this season's Class M State Champ the week before.

Every subsequent team match kind of followed in intensity to Dakota's. All of our wrestlers fought hard against stiff competition more experienced than them. None of our boys got pinned. And that's something to be very proud of. Out of the nine matches we wrestled, we won five of them, and a few of them were by pins, too. We had started out down 24 points. We then outwrestled Bristol and only lost the meet by nine points.

Once again, we lost but won. Well, at least in my eyes, we did.

Thursday's practice went well. We worked on some underhooks and ankle picks, among other things. An ice storm moved in on Friday, and school and sports were canceled again. This practice cancellation gave us an extra pound for Saturday's weigh-in. We coaches also gave a direct order to the kids to work out on their own on Friday and be on weight for Saturday.

There were a lot of ups and downs on Saturday. One of the ups was having the Enfield Coach, Paul Diaz, the South Windsor Coach, Judd Knapp, and I, all old wrestling teammates from East Hartford, at the same team tournament. Paul suggested that we three old warriors take a picture together for nostalgia's sake. After the photo was snapped, someone yelled, "That picture is going to be worth some money." It was a great picture, even if my hair was a bit messy from showing some wrestling moves that day.

Our first match was against Newington High School. Like us, they had holes in their lineup, and both of our teams traded forfeits with each other. Dakota and our team both won against

Newington. But Dakota looked flat during the mat wrestling portion of the match. I told him to play the takedown game for the third period, take his opponent down, and let him up. Then, take him down again and let him up. I figured Dakota would eventually get the kid to land on his side and then be able to turn him to his back. Or he'd eventually point the kid out from wrestling on his feet. Well, Dakota took me literally and took the kid down, let him up. Then took him down again and let him up. But after the next takedown, he just rode the kid again for the rest of the match. I guess my son didn't understand what the takedown game really is. Another assumption I think I shouldn't have made. And another reminder of how inexperienced Dakota really is in this sport.

Next, we wrestled South Windsor. They are a good team. My old teammate, Jude Knapp, is a great coach. Plus, they have a great youth feeder program. That's the same youth program our head coach, Coach Corrente used to coach before he came to Mansfield to coach our high school team. The South Windsor boy Dakota was supposed to wrestle was a former state champ but didn't wrestle because of a concussion. So, Dakota got a forfeit and didn't wrestle against South Windsor. However, South Windsor has two independent wrestlers from Tolland who don't have a wrestling program or their own. After we lost to South Windsor, the two Tolland boys got a crack at Dakota and our 145-pounder.

Dakota beat his opponent from Tolland 10-1. And Tolland's 145-pounder, Evan Albert, the son of East Hartford's head coach, and my old buddy and teammate, Todd Albert, pinned our 145-pounder. Todd couldn't be at the match to watch his son because he was coaching his own team, East Hartford, at a different location. But his wife, Kim, and his daughter Paige were there rooting for Evan. Watching Evan Albert and Dakota Blanchard wrestle back-to-back in this meet brought back memories of their fathers (Todd and me) wrestling back-to-back when we were their age. Todd Albert and I had stood side-by-side wrestled back-to-back in the Connecticut State Championship Finals 30 plus years ago... On what many consider the best East Hartford wrestling team ever... Todd and I had won many matches together back in the day. And now I got to witness both Dakota and Evan wrestle back-to-back and walk away victorious just like their fathers did so many times so many years ago.

Next, we wrestled Northwestern. Sadly, Covid has decimated their team, and they actually gave us more forfeits than we gave them. Like many of his teammates, Dakota received one of those forfeits and didn't wrestle. After wrestling just a few matches, we were declared the victor.

Our last match of the night was against Hall High School. This was a very frustrating one that we lost. Many things went wrong for us, and it seemed like none of our kids could catch a break. In addition, the referee certainly didn't help us out any. As I've told my kids before, never leave the match in the referee's hands. Unfortunately, a few of our wrestlers did, and they paid the price for that, including Dakota.

Dakota's opponent was a pretty good wrestler. But, regardless, Dakota outwrestled him. Dakota made a few mistakes, like giving his competitor an easy escape near the out-of-bounds line and committing a few penalties. Near the end of the match, Dakota scored five points, and the other boy scored only one real point on his own. Dakota was riding his opponent hard but got warned for stalling. The referee thought Dakota was spending too much time on his opponent's hips. Later in the second period, the kid ran out of bounds. The referee erroneously nailed Dakota for a stalling point, saying Dakota pushed his opponent out of bounds. That wasn't even close to being true. At the beginning of the third period, Dakota's hands accidentally touched for a fraction of a second while riding the kid. The referee called locked hands, giving Dakota's opponent another point. Then the other kid stood up and ran out of bounds again. The referee nailed Dakota for two more penalty points for stalling, saying that Dakota pushed him out of bounds. Again that wasn't even close to being true. These terrible calls caused the match to be tied up 5-5 with 30 seconds left, even though it should have been 5-0.

With about 15 seconds left in the match, Dakota's opponent scored his first truly earned point by escaping and taking a 6-5 lead. Dakota worked desperately in the last 10 seconds to secure a takedown and win. But it didn't happen as the boy kept running away from him. Dakota lost the match 6-5. It was a hard loss to swallow. But... that's life sometimes... life and wrestling are full of disappointments like this one, and we have to pick up our heads, learn from it, and go on.

And go on we will... Hopefully, Dakota won't put another match in the hands of the referee.

Brian Preece: That last loss Dakota suffered is excruciating. And I'm sure Coach and Dad are taking it harder than Dakota. I know Dakota will learn from it and bounce back. Though Dakota outwrestled his opponent, it was apparent his opponent was a good enough athlete to stay in the match. And, with a few questionable calls, turn defeat into victory. I think Dakota will learn not to be as careless about giving up points, which is a good lesson before the state meet.

That match did revive a memory of a dual meet that we lost by one point in a very controversial manner. It was against the school that would end up taking state. They had more star power than we did, so I knew we wouldn't take state and that they probably would. But they were vulnerable in a dual meet because they had a couple of holes in their line-up where we put up a solid wrestler in every weight class.

This school, Pleasant Grove, was also where my Dad's rival Darold Henry once coached, and he was the athletic director at the time of this meet. It was in January of 1997, and one of the last times my father would see me coach. And he and his rival (and friend) would have some words one last time. Let's just say Dad wasn't happy with how the events went where he felt there was some "home cooking" that "screwed over" his son's team. Dads will be Dads.

It wasn't totally the official, who is a good friend of mine. In one match, he could have called stalling against the Pleasant Grove wrestler that might have given our wrestler a chance to win in overtime. As fate would have it, their wrestler would finish second in state, and we would finish third. But the next match at 152 pounds, we were winning the match by a single point. The house was packed, even we bought a good contingent of fans. It was deafening in the arena when the buzzer went off. The official didn't hear the buzzer, and their kid shot a double leg and took our guy down. Then a conference was held at the scorer's table. The Pleasant Grove wrestler was awarded the takedown and the victory, which proved critical to the dual outcome. And yes, the video showed that the takedown came way after the buzzer. But video can't be used to determine the results in high school matches (they do have video replay in college matches and allow coaches challenges). But this isn't an option in high school wrestling.

It so happened that these two wrestlers would square off again at the region meet, and our wrestler would win by three or four points. Oh well, but maybe a lesson was learned by our wrestler that was applied later.

The matches progressed, and at 215 pounds, we were down 11 points. We knew we were getting a forfeit victory at 285 pounds. And our 215-pounder was pretty good. He would take fourth in state that year and then take state the following year, too. Their guy knew what he needed to do, and that was not get pinned. Our wrestler pressed the action maybe too much and gave up a few points but settled in and built up a good lead after a while. But then, in the final parts of the second round and all the third round, the Pleasant Grove wrestler curled up in basically the fetal position. Our crowd, and I, were going nuts wanting points for stalling, and some stall calls were made, but the last one that would disqualify the wrestler outright and give us the six-point victory was not.

During the match, I debated in that third round whether we should try to cut (loose) the wrestler and try to score enough points to get at least a technical fall. That would have tied the dual. But we didn't go that path as I thought we might turn the wrestler or get that last stall call. It didn't happen. We won the match by 12 points, but that was just a major decision or four team points. It pulled us within seven points, and then with the forfeit win at 285 pounds, we ended up losing by one. Back in 1997, there weren't any criteria like there is now to determine the winner of the dual if it was tied. A tie was a tie. So I gambled, I guess, and went for the win.

The whole night wasn't a shining example of good coaching and perspective for me. During the jayvee matches, I got so upset with that official, also a friend of mine, and I tossed a chair. It wasn't quite Bobby Knight style, but I threw it backwards into the brick wall, maybe ten feet behind me. And my principal was sitting close by with their principal. A week later, I got an official reprimand from our region and was put on probation. I deserved it.

By the time the varsity matches rolled around, I was in quite the lather. And the matches were quite intense, and the crowd was revved up, and with a series of things going against our team, our crowd got extremely hostile, my father among them. It was on the cusp of being really a bad scene, but thankfully it didn't go beyond jawing. I think my poor Mom was mortified at her son's behavior and that of her husband.

Our dual meet was covered by the county newspaper. And I went off saying how "they stole the dual meet away from our boys" or something to that effect. Heidi, now my wife but my fiancé back then, consoled me after the meet. So glad she was there. Much of what happened after the meet, what I said to my team, if anything, is a blur. I was so upset and angry that I forgot some things about that night. This is probably a good thing.

The next day I was at home at my condo when I got a phone call. It was from Leroy Adamson, their assistant coach. Leroy was a good friend, and my parents had actually bought a car or two from him when he worked for one of Larry Miller's car dealerships. (Larry Miller was also the longtime owner of the Utah Jazz). I expected him to tear into me about what I said in the papers or any number of things I did that night. But instead, he actually consoled me and wanted to make sure that I was okay and that we were okay. I thought that was a nice gesture.

I guess I still get a bit upset (and regretful) thinking about that dual meet some 25 years ago. I know we wouldn't beat these guys at the region and state tournaments, but beating them in a dual meet would be a good feather in the cap, so to speak, for our program. It would have meant that we went undefeated in our region dual meets. I think it would have been cool for my Dad to see a Preece beat Pleasant Grove one last time before he passed away. We would get that dual meet win two seasons later against our rival, but it was a battle of teams that would finish in the back end of the top ten versus two teams that would finish first and fourth in the state meet. But it was still nice anyway.

Yes, I could be a fiery coach. But I think a coach should fight for his boys. I don't think I had a bad reputation or anything with other coaches or officials, but I was just one that would fight for his boys and sometimes maybe go a bit too far. I lost five or six team points in 33 years of coaching (12 as a head coach), got tossed from one dual meet, and had a couple "letters in my file." But I hope I did more than good than not, especially with the officials. As I said, the varsity and jayvee officials in that meet were friends. And I would often request them for tournaments we ran, ensuring I showed gratitude for their efforts. The varsity official even admitted that maybe he made mistakes and was unsettled a bit by the large and emotional crowd.

So back to Daniel and Dakota, the official probably did screw up. And sometimes officials make mistakes, even costly mistakes. But they are humans like the rest of us. It still doesn't make the loss any easier, though.

Chapter 11

NO "SENIOR NIGHT" FOR DAKOTA

Dan Blanchard: This week began with some bizarre injuries. We had nine wrestlers at both of our Monday and Tuesday night practices. However, Monday night's injuries made it difficult for some of us, including myself, to do much on Tuesday night.

Monday at practice, our 160-pounder reaggravated his rib injury. Our 126-pounder had a big bump on his wrist and arm that none of us could seem to explain. Another wrestler moved to the side and grabbed a bag of ice for something else that hurt. Also, my right pinkie hand finger twisted and bent somehow. And no matter how hard I tried to turn it and bend it back, it just wouldn't cooperate and go back into the correct position. Now my hand is wrapped up, and I'm waiting to get an appointment with a hand specialist sometime next week.

On Tuesday, a few more kids came into practice telling me they got hurt the day before and couldn't do much for that practice. I pulled the team in and announced that when they get hurt, they need to tell us coaches right away so we can try to do something about it. Dakota then made a joke that he was hurt all over. We all laughed, but we all also knew that he was telling the truth, and there really wasn't much we could do for him. Dakota is just going to have to suck it up and get through the state tournament. After states, he can rest and heal.

For some reason, all of our home wrestling meets were at the beginning of the season. So, now we're scrambling, trying to put together a wrestling meet for Saturday to have a Senior Day. We want an opportunity to honor our wrestlers who will be graduating and their families, as well. So far, we have been unsuccessful. Hopefully, something works out this week. Our kids have had a lot of meets canceled due to Covid, and now they may not have a Senior Day/Night as well.

It's looking more and more like Wednesday night against Windsor may be our last regular season meet. There are still no takers for Saturday to have a Senior Appreciation Day. We boarded ten wrestlers and a wrestling manager onto the 4:00 P.M. bus Wednesday night for Windsor. I told Coach Corrente that I believe this is the biggest team we've had so far on the bus. He looked back at the kids and smiled.

Windsor's meet went well. My sister, Rosie, who works in Windsor, came to watch Dakota wrestle. The night's matches started off at 152-pounds, which should have been Dakota. But, it wasn't because we bumped up a good part of our team to the next weight class. So, our 145-pounder wrestled the first match of the night at the 152-pound weight class.

Our boy wrestled tough, and it was an exhilarating match. He had the Windsor boy gasping for air and just trying to survive out there against him. Sadly, the match ended with our boy being one point short and thus the loser. Later that night, when my sister came out of the stands, she informed me how the coaches missed a two-point move that our kid did and didn't get the points for. Later that night, at home, Coach Rogers went back and watched the video and saw what my sister said. Our boy was robbed out of two points that, for some reason, didn't get recorded. He should have won that match. I can't believe that all three of us coaches missed that one. We feel terrible that we didn't protect our boy from being robbed of a win he had earned.

Dakota came up next. He wrestled up at the 160-pound weight class, dominating his opponent. Dakota was never in any trouble and beat the kid 11-0. I don't think the kid ever came close to scoring. But, the boy did stall, similar to the Windsor kid from the previous match. Our wrestlers were definitely in better shape than the Windsor kids were.

The 170-pound match was pretty cool. We bumped our 160-pounder up to 170. There, he went against a female opponent from Windsor who was a four-year wrestler and the captain of their team. This was the first time in my life that I've ever seen a female wrestling captain. So, this was pretty cool, and I much admired her. And I told her so when she came over to shake hands with me. Later, my sister said to me that she was rooting for the girl and was sad when our boy beat her. You see, my sister wanted to wrestle back in the late 80s, but East Hartford coach Steve Konopka wouldn't allow it. So, she had to settle on being the wrestling manager instead.

Some of the matches that followed were good, and a few weren't so good for us. However, our team wrestled well enough to pull off a comfortable win and was never in trouble of losing. The bus ride home was a joyous one. We had won. We won convincingly, and we were all happy about it.

However, still no luck on getting anyone to wrestle us on the upcoming Saturday. I feel bad for our seniors. They won't have a Senior Day this year. Hopefully, we can make up for it at our end-of-the-season wrestling celebration.

Without a meet on Saturday, we went a little easier in practice on Thursday. I showed some techniques in a few areas that I noticed need improvement. Our boys have been dropping their knee to the mat during scrambles and even sprawls and giving up two points that they shouldn't be giving up. We also mixed up the workout by hitting the weight room and getting the boys out of practice on time. I'm sure parents waiting in the parking lot were happy about this last one.

Since we didn't have a meet on Saturday and my oldest daughter needed to be up at Logan Airport in Boston at the same time we practice on Friday, Dakota and I did something we hadn't done yet this season. We both took the night off, with the blessings of the other coaches and the team, to go to Boston's airport. My oldest daughter is going to South Korea for a semester abroad. I couldn't be more proud of her. And I was happy that wrestling worked out in a way that allowed both Dakota and I to be there when she boarded her plane to leave us for the next five months.

We miss her already. And now Dakota's high school wrestling career is nearing an end too. And I'm pretty sure that eventually, we're going to miss all this craziness and hardship that wrestling has brought us over the last four years. But, in the meantime, here come the post-season wrestling tournaments. And now we have to get ready for them. But first, I need to shovel our 460-foot dirt driveway out again from another snowstorm in time to watch the Super Bowl LVI.

Brian Preece: I feel bad that Dakota and his teammates didn't get a Senior Night. I look back at mine, and it was about as eventful as almost nothing. I can't remember any big recognition, but we did do an afternoon dual. My Dad was hoping that we could draw some kind of crowd by moving the dual to right after school. Most of the time, crowds were Spartan and limited to a small group of parents in a very large spacious gym, making the crowd feel even smaller. But somehow, we got something worked out with the basketball coach and the opposing team to have our dual in the afternoon. Incidentally, it was against Cyprus, where my Dad coached before he came over to Skyline. A few of their wrestlers still knew my Dad or knew of him. The junior high coach took over for my Dad, and I knew him pretty well. He coached well into my own coaching career. So we had a "Senior Day," I guess because the dual started at 3:00 p.m. in the afternoon.

I remember my Dad bumping me up a weight. I didn't know why as we had a 155-pounder, but he yelled at me, "Don't you want a match on your Senior Day?" I nodded my head affirmatively. They didn't have a 145-pounder, so my friend and teammate Mark Hult, a junior on our team, gave up his match so I could have one on "Senior Day." I remember as I warmed up looking over at my opponent. I didn't know who he was, but he looked a lot bigger than me and very athletic. Now the pressure was on, I had to win this match in front of a bigger crowd of our students than I ever remember having in any previous meet. I won the match comfortably, something like 12-0. He was strong but didn't have a lot of wrestling skills. The only hairy thing was late in the match I got my arm caught in a weird situation in the third round. My Dad got loud, the official stopped the match, and all was good. I avoided a possible injury before the region (or state qualifying) meet the next week.

We still lost the dual by a good margin, but I was glad that I won in front of some of my classmates, many of whom were on the basketball team. The guy I wrestled looked pretty strong, so I looked tough enough and enjoyed their praise and that of the basketball coach, who I had as a P.E. teacher. I liked him, and he ran an excellent program. He's in the Utah Sports Hall of Fame like my father. He later would coach my younger brother on the golf team. So I guess the Senior Day sort of worked out okay. The audience was larger than normal because we had people hanging around after school, mostly basketball players waiting to practice and football players around for weight-lifting.

As a coach, I know I tried to do more for my seniors than I remember my coach doing. Before the match, and sometimes I did it after to see how that went, we would honor the seniors by calling them out to the center of the mat with their parents. I would say something nice, Mom would get a flower, and so forth. I did more for them at the banquet. But we also recognized the managers, the coach's wives or girlfriends, the athletic director, the athletic trainer. We encouraged them to bring their spouses or significant others.

I know I was really hustling to get flowers between the time school let out and the weigh-in, which was usually 4:30 p.m. I would also have a program for every wrestling meet, and I would do it during some free time in my classes or my prep period and then get it to the copy center. I also took care of Margaret Craft, who ran the copy center, because she took care of me very well. We always had a school policy of getting any documents for anything that needed to be copied 24 hours in advance. Still, she always made the exception for me and often, on her own, did the programs in nicer card stock. She was one of those unsung heroes of that "village" that made my life easier, so I could be a better teacher and coach. But more importantly, she was one of those school employees that were plotting to get a young lady and me together. And it worked, and that young lady (Heidi) became my wife.

I would always try to email the opposing coach the night before or in the morning to get their line-ups. I know some coaches didn't want to play along, or they were planning on shifting weights like what happened with Dakota, so I did my best. But every home meet, I did a program that talked about the accomplishments of the wrestlers that week. Of course, the Senior Night one was a bit more voluminous.

Over time, athletic teams go all out with blankets for the seniors. My sister really, really went all out for her volleyball team. They have an indoor track at their school that goes around the bleachers, and the gym is below the track. But on the upper concourse, she'll have tables set up for each senior. I think she works with the Moms, and they put together a table with photos and keepsakes. Each of the seniors will also get a nice vinyl poster of themselves. Then she has a gigantic vinyl poster made of the entire senior class put up in a prominent place in the gym. Then before the game, she'll introduce all the seniors, and they march out with their parents to get more gifts like a bouquet of flowers and balloons. Then according to my Mom, who often attends the banquet, things really get serious with the tributes and more gifts. So by the end of their volleyball experience, each senior gets at least a plaque, large action poster, flowers, and flowers for their Mom, and an embroidered blanket.

I do remember I had a bunch of seniors I really loved. To me, they were a special class with some team leaders that were captains for multiple years. They were crucial in bringing our program back from some more challenging years with their outstanding leadership. I knew there was no way I was not going to tear up. And while they looked at me, they'd probably get emotional. Or Mom and Dad would get emotional, or some combination thereof, and that might not be good before going into combat. So I did the Senior Night recognition after the meet, just asking our fans to wait a little bit as the visiting crowd left. Then we did our thing, and yes, tears were shed. And that was more than fine.

Chapter 12

GUTTING IT OUT!

Dan Blanchard: In some ways, many years, it seems like week 12 leading up to the Class State Championship weekend tournament feels like the hardest one every year. There is so much anticipation over where our wrestlers, or our sons, will rank in the mid-week coaches seeding meeting. Many of us are tired of being tired and hurt. Some of us become disappointed in how the coaches' seeding meeting values us and places us in their ranking system for the tournament. Then some of us can't believe it's almost over and are feeling that bittersweet pain of nostalgia already. And then there are others whose minds are torturing them because they can see the finish line but aren't there yet. Those individuals just want the season to be over, but then will be sad and miss it when it is over... It's not easy to always feel good in this sport of wrestling. Unfortunately, there are way too many ways to feel bad about how things are going. It's a real mental game right now for many of us in the wrestling community...

I'm feeling a little down myself. In my mind, I had envisioned myself live wrestling with my son Dakota and the two of us really going at it near the end of the season. I imagined that we'd have some great brawls and that I'd do a lot to help him peak and be ready for the state tournament. Unfortunately, this didn't happen, and I feel like I let Dakota down some. Among some other injuries, I just added a messed-up finger. The doctor said I can't bend it for six weeks if I want it to heal. Nor should I be wrestling. So, now Dakota and the rest of his teammates have to just settle for me showing them and telling them what moves to do instead of wrestling with me. It saddens me to end the season of Dakota's senior year with this sort of hands-off approach.

Also, at the beginning of this week, our starting 182-pounder came to practice with his arm in a sling. It turns out that he dislocated his shoulder wrestling last week. Surprisingly, he asked me to wrestle in the Class M State Tournament this upcoming weekend. Thankfully, all three of us coaches were on the same page when we told him, "No." We also said that his job was to heal, get well, have a good summer and fall football season, and then be ready to wrestle again next winter.

Our head coach, Bill Corrente, went to the coaches' seeding meeting in Cheshire on Tuesday. Coach Rogers and I stayed back to run practice. I thought it would be better if Coach Rogers and I took a half of a step back and played more of a supportive role. We encouraged Dakota to step up as the senior captain and run practice himself.

Dakota running practice with the coaches there to help him was great for his self-esteem going into the States. Dakota had some great ideas on what he thought the team needed. He is a great wrestler and very knowledgeable. Dakota might even someday make a great wrestling coach if he ever chooses to.

Similar to how I promised myself that I'd never force him to wrestle, I won't force him to coach someday either. However, he did an excellent job planning and running practice with only some minor help from Coach Rogers and me. I firmly believe Dakota will make a great coach someday if that's what he wants to be...

We went a little harder during the early parts of this week. I even pulled a big garbage basket up to the side of the mat, just in case. And I guess it was a good move because we had kids huddling around the garbage can on both Monday and Tuesday a few times. No one actually threw up, but a few looked like they might have been close. It reminded me of the old days when we had tough wrestling practices. In the old days, the difference was that we actually did throw up in the baskets and then went right back to practice.

Furthermore, we weren't allowed water breaks in the old days like we do today. In the old days, coaches showed no mercy. If you broke, then you didn't belong there.

Even among the tough wrestling practices that we had on Monday and Tuesday night, I couldn't help but hear the wrestlers occasionally joking around and laughing at different times. There was a long moment when I paused and really took in the kids' laughter. During that moment, I told myself, "I'm going to miss hearing these young men laugh. Dakota is sore all over and looking forward to a break, but I know Dakota will miss all this too. He, too, will miss hearing the laughter coming from his wrestling teammates.

Coach Corrente was back in practice on Wednesday. However, instead of starting practice in our usual way, Coach had invited parents to the beginning of our practice. He did a little awards ceremony where he and his wife made up some beautiful award certificates for every kid on the team for different things. As we passed out the various awards, Coach Corrente let the individual wrestler and the parents know the kid's record and the number he seeded for the state tournament.

Dakota was awarded the Wrestling Team Leader, and he was seeded 5th in the Class M State Tournament. I didn't argue with the seeding, but deep down in my heart, I knew he was good enough to be seeded number two or maybe three. A few things just didn't go his way this year. Oh, well... I guess that's just how life goes, especially a wrestler's life.

At the end of the ceremony, we took a picture of all the wrestlers on the mat with all the team parents standing behind them, which I thought was pretty cool. Some of the parents then stayed and watched our wrestling practice that followed. Thankfully, no one needed the trash bucket that night. I've never done a wrestling practice with an awards ceremony like this before. It was different and kind of neat. Coach Corrente thinks he might make a team tradition of this combination of an awards ceremony, announcing the seeding, and then doing a practice that parents can watch. And I think it might be a good idea.

Thursday's practice, the last one before states, went well. We went lighter and did a lot of drilling. At the end of practice, Coach Corrente, Dakota, and I, like always, stayed after and made sure everything was cleaned up and put away. Then the three of us, like always, walked up the long hallway leading from the back gym to the school's front door. And once again, Coach Corrente joked about Dakota leaving the school in pajama pants and no jacket. The three of us have done this routine so many times that it just seems like it's something we're supposed to do forever.

However, this is the last time we'll ever do this routine. Next week, our few kids who place and move forward will team up and practice at a neighboring school with other kids going to the State Open. I'm going to miss those long walks up the E.O. Smith hallway leaving the building that Coach, Dakota, and I have been taking every night. And on the other end, I guess I'll also miss the time Dakota, and I spent together at the beginning of each practice rolling out the mats.

The Class M Wrestling State Championships were wild and exhausting this past weekend. There were so many ups and downs. While our kids wrestled 3-6 matches, our coaching staff felt like it wrestled in every one of those matches of every one of our wrestlers. These weekends are one of the most challenging things anyone can imagine. But, at the same time, it's also one of the most exciting things anyone can experience. And I feel so lucky to have done these types of weekends more times in my life than I can count.

Want to hear something really cool? Even though our E.O. Smith wrestling team showed up with only half a team to the Class M State Championship against 28 teams, we walked away two days later with 11th place. That is amazing! Our 126-pounder took 2nd. Our heavyweight took 3rd. And Dakota, at 152-pounds, took 4th. Our other four varsity wrestlers all made it to the blood round. They were all winning or on the verge of winning when something happened that snatched victory from them. We are so proud of those four young inexperienced boys who really stepped up and wrestled their hearts out. We couldn't have asked any more of them. If a couple of things had gone differently, they all would have somehow found their way into the medal rounds.

Dakota started off as usual, nervous and a bit shaky. After getting a bye, I thought he'd beat the next guy up, but nerves got him a little bit, and he was a bit sloppy and struggled some. Eventually, Dakota pinned the kid and moved on to the quarterfinals. There, he met a talented wrestler from Avon who was very well-coached by John McLaughlin. John and I wrestled each other in the semifinals of the State Open Championship in 1988. He was a great wrestler and is a great coach. So, I knew the Avon kid would be tough, and the match would be very close. However, I figured Dakota would win it by a score of 5-3 or maybe 4-2.

Dakota, again, had a slow start and went down 2-0. Again his nerves were shaking him up some and making him a bit sloppy out there. To his credit, Dakota did go on the attack and tried very hard to get on the scoreboard. Dakota got back to his feet and continuously shot on the Avon boy. But the Avon boy kept successfully defending himself with good sprawls and a good front headlock. All season long, I've been on Dakota about dragging out of those front headlocks, and for some strange unknown reason, he just doesn't do it. I don't know why he doesn't do it. He just doesn't.

I think the Avon boy only shot once the entire match against Dakota. And Dakota shut him down when he did. I would say that Dakota shot on the Avon boy seven or more times, and each one of those times, I yelled myself hoarse to Dakota to drag out and get his points. At one point, Coach West from KT KIDZ, who Dakota trained with in the fall, ran over to my side and yelled to Dakota to double up on the kid's elbow (to drag out).

So, I stopped yelling, hoping that the new voice might have a positive effect. Unfortunately, it didn't because Dakota couldn't hear us. Dakota wrestled hard, but in the end, he lost 4-2. I was heartbroken. I should have known the Avon kid would wrestle a defensive match against Dakota, just like his coach tried to do to me all those years ago. I dropped the ball on this one as my son's wrestling coach.

I thought Dakota was the better wrestler and should have won that match. Even though the Avon kid was seeded one spot ahead of Dakota as #4, I still felt like it was an upset. In my mind, the better kid lost. So, it was an upset. However, on the other side of the coin, I had to pay homage to the Avon boy and his Coach, my old comrade John McLaughlin, for doing what they had to do to win. Way to go, Avon, on a hard-fought victory.

I went to bed Friday night, psychologically shaken up. My heart was breaking. I had to find a way to pull myself back together. And I knew Dakota must have been going through the same thing. He was going to have to make a huge decision. Was Dakota going to fall apart and feel sorry for himself, knowing that now he couldn't be a Class M State Champ? Or was Dakota going to step up and do everything we've been talking about for the last few years of facing and overcoming adversity as a real man should?

Saturday morning, he stepped on the mat in a must-win situation. He looked okay to me, but only time would tell if his mind was right or not. Dakota got the first takedown and then proceeded to tear up his opponent. His mind was right! It was some of the best wrestling I had seen from him all season. After Dakota's match, I watched the Avon boy come from behind and pull off a massive upset by beating the #1 seed in their weight class in the semifinals. The Avon boy caught the Waterford boy in a front headlock and then used the head chancery to put him to his hip and then his back for a pin. The arena went wild with that colossal upset! Well done again, Avon and my old comrade, Coach McLaughlin.

Dakota soon stepped on the mat again in another must-win situation in the blood round. When he came over to the coaches' corner to put on his green ankle band, he looked me in the eye and said, "I've worked too hard to let this kid keep me from med-aling." I replied, "You're right! You've earned this! Now go take it!" At that moment, my heart was put at ease. As far as I was concerned, the match result was already foreordained. Dakota went out there and tore that kid up.

The same exact thing happened in the next round that would decide if Dakota wrestled for 3rd or 5th later that night. Dakota went out there with confidence that he had earned the right to fight for third, and he tore up his opponent. He even pinned his guy early in the second period. It was a dominating performance by Dakota. What a day he was having!

Dakota went into the consolation finals to fight for third with a full head of steam. He was going against the #1 seed upset by the Avon boy when he caught him in the front headlock and then head chancery. In the Lancer Tournament, this same #1 seed Waterford boy pinned Dakota early in the first period a few months ago. The thought of wrestling this kid again for 3rd must have been scary for Dakota. However, this was not the same Dakota that this kid pinned a couple months ago. Dakota's mind was right today, and he was coming off of three dominating performances.

The referee blew the whistle, and the Waterford boy immediately attacked. Dakota defended himself well. However, after several more attacks, the Waterford boy got in deep and secured a takedown against Dakota. The first period ended with the Waterford boy up 2-0. This was much better than how the first period went the last time these two boys wrestled. This was shaping up to be a good match.

Dakota picked down in the second period. The Waterford boy was relentless on top, and he rode the heck out of Dakota like a turtle shell that couldn't be knocked off. Dakota had difficulty staying off his back, let alone getting out from underneath the Waterford boy's attacks. The second period ended still at 2-0. Nobody expected this match to be this close after two periods. This in itself was a victory for Dakota.

Third period, the Waterford kid picked down and escaped, making it 3-0. After some rough hand-fighting, the Waterford wrestler took Dakota down again, making it 5-0. Again, he rode Dakota hard and gave Dakota a lot of trouble. As time ticked down, I screamed from the coaching corner at the top of my lungs for Dakota to stand and throw him. Somehow, Dakota got to his feet and got the escape, making it 5-1, and went on the attack immediately. The Waterford wrestler backed out of bounds to stop Dakota's aggressive attack.

As they headed back to the center of the mat to restart the match with only nine seconds left, I screamed to Dakota, You have nothing left to lose! Headlock him right to his back to win this match! The whistle blew, and Dakota went after his opponent with fire in his eyes. The Waterford wrestler who had dominated Dakota the first time they wrestled ran backward away from Dakota, denying him his Hail Mary headlock victory. Time ran out, and Dakota couldn't headlock him for the big come from behind win.

However, even though Dakota lost to this kid again, compared to how the first match went, this one was kind of gratifying. This time it was kind of nice to see Dakota's opponent, who would go on and take second in the State Open, backpedaling for his life to get away from Dakota as the match ended. Dakota lost 5-1 and didn't get the victory or 3rd place, but he certainly had a championship performance that Saturday at Class M States! And he certainly did earn the respect of this Waterford kid, and I assume his coach, too.

A quick side note here. I just heard that my alma mater, East Hartford High School, just tied long-time powerhouse Danbury High School for first place in the LL State Championship Tournament. East Hartford is co-state champs with Danbury. Also, my old buddy and classmate, Kelly Boyd, her son, placed and will be going to the State Open. Maybe her son, Cooper, and my son Dakota will get a chance to meet up and wrestle before this season is over, after all. We're both betting on our own sons to win if that should happen.

Brian Preece: That was cool to see Dakota place at the Class M state tournament. If I understand things, he moves on to the Open State tournament. In Utah, we have six classifications (way too many). The 26 larger schools are (6A), and the next largest 33 schools are (5A). Our 4A classification has 13 schools, and our 3A has 20 schools, while both the 1A and 2A each have 13 schools.

We have a weekend invitational that is tougher than some of our state tournaments most of the time. In fact, we have several tournaments way more demanding than any of our state tournaments. But of course, "taking state" is a big deal. Dakota has a chance to do that. And to take state, first, you have to be in the tournament, and I am happy Dakota qualified. Then if he can place high enough there, he can move on to the New England championships. This includes the states of Connecticut, Maine, Massachusetts, New Hampshire, Rhode Island, and Vermont. I wonder if Utah could team up with states like Colorado, Idaho, Montana, New Mexico, Nevada, and Wyoming for some Intermountain championship. That would be way cool. I know Utah put a team together to take on Idaho in the past, but it was just for fun, nothing official on the line.

We also had four classifications for our girl wrestlers. This year, the 4A, 5A, and 6A had their own classifications and the 1A-3A combined. Just over 600 girl wrestlers competed in those four tournaments. That is totally exciting. I wouldn't say I was a pioneer in girls wrestling, but certainly an early advocate. I used the power of the pen, so to speak, to show my support, and I was on the staff that coached the first two high school girl wrestlers in the state, and in Utah County, I coached the first three female wrestlers. They took a lot of garbage, some from their teammates sadly, but to see 600 girls go at it now, a generation later, is so cool.

We did the boys' state tournaments alongside the girls' state tournaments. This year, we were back doing our state tournaments in college arenas. Last year because of COVID-19, we were in high school gyms, and each classification held its own state tournament. It wasn't the best way to inaugurate the first official state tournament in girls wrestling, but we did it right this year. It was neat to see, and I take a small amount of pride in my role to make it happen.

When Daniel told me what Coach Corrente did in their final practice, I thought that was really cool. I know they didn't really have a Senior Night for their team because of COVID-19 and some scheduling quirks. These nice gestures by the Coach will be remembered, and I thought involving the parents was a nice touch.

When I was the head coach at Provo High School, we also had a tradition of sorts, though it was just between coaches and athletes. We did it the Monday after the region tournament with those that qualified for the state tournament.

Overlooking our gym was a room we called the "Crow's Nest." It was supposed to be an area where coaches could gather to watch games, but maybe it didn't have the best location because it really didn't serve that function as we all had hoped. I used it to run wrestling tournaments. I personally liked to watch basketball games there even if nobody really joined me. But the room served another purpose for our wrestling team. It was the room where we kicked off our preparation for the state meet.

I would prepare a packet of sorts and put the contents in a manila envelope with each wrestler's name on them. The wrestlers were told to go to the Crow's Nest before practice. Before the meeting, I would strategically move the couches a bit if needed to generally face me. The packet I gave them included the practice schedule and information for the state tournament that their parents might find helpful. I put such things as; weigh-in times, when the wrestling started, spectator cost, etc.). I might have put in a gift or token of some sort, but I think the most important thing I put in there was a letter.

I told them I was proud of them in this letter, and I thanked them for their work. Then I gave some advice. Some advice was on diet and supplements (I told them not to change their diet because Uncle Fred said they should take bee pollen or extra Vitamin B-12 or something). I told them about the "1-2-3-4 principle." The 1-2-3-4 principle was that one comes before two and two before three and three before four, and it simply meant you had to win match one before you got to match two. The wrestlers were told they were only to focus on the match ahead of them, not the possible matches ahead. But I told them with this caveat. We, as coaches, would be looking ahead and scouting their possible opponents and gleaning information from other sources. But they needed to focus only on the match in front of them.

I also told them flatly that some of them might lose, but if they were to lose, I desired they pick themselves up and battle back because placing in state is better than not placing in state. And oftentimes, in consolation matches at state, it wasn't the better wrestler or athlete, or even the wrestler in better condition, that would win the match. Sometimes it was simply the one that wanted it more, that was willing to keep fighting when their big dream was dashed, the one that truly had a positive outlook.

Further, I suggested they keep their routines as normal as possible. I also told them to surround themselves with positive people who believed in them. And this might be controversial for some, but I told them they should avoid negative people for the next few days. Sadly, that might be family members, even their Mom or Dad. I also told them that they needed to listen to their coaches first and foremost, again something that people might find offensive or whatever. But I said we were the ones working with them every day in practice. We knew their strengths and weaknesses as wrestlers best in regards to technique. I was very blunt on those issues.

I usually gave my assistant coaches some time to speak. We would share some inspirational stories or just words of wisdom. And my main assistant Darren Hirsche always had plenty of wisdom. I was always proud that we as a staff would edify each other and edify each other, especially in front of the athletes. I was on many coaching staffs where that wasn't the case where coaches often made fun of other coaches or did things to make kids doubt the knowledge of the other coaches. I hated that and made sure that didn't happen on my coaching staff. I would never do anything to belittle my coaches in any way. I needed my wrestlers to know that I had complete faith in my coaching staff, and they could trust them to coach them correctly. This is important because we used four or five mats at our state tournament, and I might not literally be in their corner when they wrestled. They had to have complete faith in all of us on the staff.

But mostly, I wanted my wrestlers to know that we loved and cared about them. I think this can help athletes perform better when they know, whatever happens, they are loved and that we care about them as people first and foremost. I wanted them to know I was grateful to them for making this journey with me and that I was proud to be their coach. I think overall, our approach worked. We wanted, in some senses, to let our wrestlers feel the freedom to wrestle to win and not to lose, having no fear at all that we really cared about them.

Our best tournament we wrestled was most often the state tournament. There is an art to get your teams to peak at state. I know one year we only had one region champion. But the next week, we had three state champions, and one of those pinned the guy who pinned him twice in the season, including the week before at region. He was pretty distraught after that loss like he took it worse than about any wrestlers I coached, but I boldly promised him he would take state if he followed the game plan. We also let him know, no matter what, that we loved him, and that was not conditional on whether he took state. I know in my heart giving him that reassurance, along with his own determination, led to him standing on top of the podium.

Chapter 13

HAVING AN ATTITUDE OF GRATITUDE AS DAKOTA'S HIGH SCHOOL SEASON ENDS

Dan Blanchard: It's another do-or-die week, and the stakes just got a whole lot bigger. The State Open is no joke. This is where the really big Connecticut boys come out to play. Every single match will be a one-on-one war on those mats. And only the top five from each weight class will move forward to compete in the New England's the following weekend.

This week we have only three wrestlers left to compete in the State Open. So, with that small number went right next store to the adjoining town, Windham, for workouts this week. RHAM high school, led by my old East Hartford buddy Ryan Fitch, is also a great wrestling program and they too were there working out. Windham has a long history of tough kids and success, and with it being right next store to Mansfield, it was a perfect workout place for us this week.

There was no school Monday due to the long weekend being part of our February vacation. The school buildings were closed, so we had to give the wrestlers the day off, which was fine because it gave our wrestlers another day to heal from the rough tournament we were just at. That's a wrestler's life. They don't really get a real Christmas vacation or a Winter/February vacation because they have to make weight, train, and wrestle in tournaments during those times.

Tuesday, we were at Windham, but unfortunately, I had to miss practice. Instead, I had to renew my annual certification in restraint training for my job as a schoolteacher. Sadly, we've had a lot of violence in our school system, and we teachers have to be trained to restrain our students. Sad, isn't it?

However, when I did get home late Tuesday night, my wife was smiling. She greeted me with a kiss and another late dinner, as she happily told me that Dakota got a good workout that day. She had picked Dakota up from Windham, and he was drenched in sweat like he is supposed to be after a good hard productive wrestling workout. My wife told me that Dakota even put one of the coaches on his back in practice that day. Sounds like it was a great workout to me!

Wednesday, we went back to Windham for another good hard workout. Unfortunately, I had to go late and meet the team there. And most of the time that I was there watching practice, I was on my phone on an emergency Zoom call. There has been some combative and nasty politics going on right now in the media about the school system where I work. It wasn't an ideal situation for a father and a coach, but at least I got to watch my son Dakota wrestle while I was on the call. I saw Dakota beating some very good kids and getting himself another great workout that day.

After insisting that Dakota put on a clean, dry shirt before he got into my car, Dakota and I had a great coach and athlete and father and son talk on the way home. I was all warm and fuzzy inside, seeing Dakota's hair drenched and him smiling from ear to ear. He had a great workout that day, and he loved it. He was excited about the new challenging positions he had to fight out of that day. This was precisely the mental and psychological space we needed Dakota to occupy going into this really tough weekend of competition ahead of us.

Dakota asked me if I had seen the wrestling brackets during the car ride home. I cautiously answered that I had seen them. I was careful not to let Dakota know that I was a bit worried. Dakota told me that he thought he could beat the first guy. I agreed that if he wrestled well and had the mental attitude that he had at that moment, I also believe he would win that first match.

Then... Dakota brought up the possible second match. This is the one I'm worried about but trying not to let him know that I'm concerned about it. Dakota told me that if all goes well in the first match, he'll have to take on the #1 guy in his weight class for his second match. I hesitated before answering him because I knew this guy was a real hammer. He's a beast. I slowly let out that I saw that when looking at the wrestling brackets as cool-headed as I could, trying not to alarm him.

Then Dakota surprised me when he kept smiling and said he was glad he would probably get the chance to wrestle the best. His head was in the right place, and I was pumped about it but didn't want to seem too excited. I didn't want to rock him out of the zone that he was in at the moment. So, I smiled and calmly answered Dakota, "Hey, you know what? Your high school wrestling career wouldn't be complete if you didn't get the chance to wrestle the number one guy at least once before you graduated."

Dakota agreed. I'm in a good place right now, knowing that Dakota is in a good place. His mental game right now, going into the State Open, is probably better than it's been all season long. This upcoming weekend just got a whole lot more interesting. And if Dakota can keep his mental edge, who knows how far he can go...

On the wee hours of the Friday morning of the first day of the scheduled State Open Tournament, a nasty snowstorm with an ice storm to follow moved into our state. Schools canceled, and the CIAC postponed the State Open Tournament to Saturday and Sunday. The wrestlers got another pound for Saturday weigh-ins, but they'd be on their own on Friday to keep their weight down. Thankfully, all three of our wrestlers, including Dakota, made weight no problem for Saturday morning's weigh-in

Dakota wrestled in the first round against Hand, the number 5 place-winner out of the L State Championship Tournament. I knew Dakota would have to wrestle tough and have his head on right to beat this kid. As usual, Dakota got off to a slow start and gave up the first takedown. Once again, his nerves were getting the best of him. Eventually, the kid increased his lead over Dakota to 5-2.

Then, late in the match, Dakota hit the kid with a beautiful trip that looked like the kid was going right to his back. And this four, or five-point move would win the match for Dakota. Or, heck, Dakota might even pin him. But unfortunately, the kid rolled right off of his back and only gave up two points to Da-kota, making the match score 5-4. There were 33 seconds left in the match. I screamed as loud as I could for Dakota to turn him right away or let him up and take him back down for the tie and a possible win in overtime. The clock kept ticking down, and Da-kota wasn't showing much progress in turning the kid. I yelled a few times to let him up, but Dakota didn't hear me and kept try-ing to turn the kid. With less than 10 seconds left, Dakota hit a desperation turn attempt and got reversed as time elapsed. It was a hard-fought match, but we still came up short.

In the sweet sixteen round, our team's 126-pounder won, and so did my heavyweight. Our coaching staff couldn't have been happier.

The next round Dakota was back in a do-or-die situation. He had to win if he wanted to continue to wrestle in the State Open Tournament. Todd Albert, my old teammate, The Best Man at my wedding, and the head coach of East Hartford High School, son, Evan, was in the same boat, and he had already begun his match on the mat next to Dakota's. Dakota's match started, and the first period went by quick and ended 0-0. I thought Dakota looked pretty good in that first period and was never really in any trouble. I noticed on the next mat over Evan was battling hard against a very good kid and was only down 2-0 after the first period. In Dakota's second period, he really came alive. He scored from every position finishing the second period up 7-2 after multiple stoppages for the other kid's nose bleeds. Evan was down 3-1 now on the mat next to Dakota.

The third period might have been one of the longest periods I have ever experienced. It seemed like the match was stopped every 15 seconds or so to stop the other boy's nose bleeds. Dakota couldn't find a rhythm in the third period, and the other wrestler slowly fought his way back to tie it up 7-7 with only 15 seconds left in the match. During another nose bleed, we found ourselves in the position of telling Dakota that now he had to stop being tentative and he needed to attack. "Hand-fight and attack! I yelled to him as he headed once again to the center. Next door, Evan's match had ended, and I had missed the final score.

Dakota's opponent's nose bleed stopped. The referee blew the whistle, and Dakota finally attacked. After a bit of hand-fighting, Dakota got in deep and took the kid down. While what looked like a sure-takedown to win the match, his opponent did some squirming and wiggling, and the referee didn't award the takedown points right away. The buzzer went off, and the referee said that Dakota didn't establish complete control of his opponent before time elapsed.

We went into overtime, where the nose bleeds continued for his opponent, and my old buddy Todd Albert had slid up on the side of the mat to root for Dakota. Near the end of the third overtime, it was all tied up again at 10-10. The other boy shot in with 7 seconds left. Dakota sprawled and began spinning behind. His competitor fought it, and Dakota stepped over for what looked like a takedown. Then the kid popped up his head and rolled through it to come up on Dakota for his own takedown. The last two seconds of the match ticked away, and Dakota's high school wrestling career ended.

Todd approached to console me over Dakota's loss. I asked him how Evan's match ended. He told me that Evan had lost too.

Just like Dakota and Evan won matches back to back earlier in the season at the South Windsor Tournament. Today they both just ended their high school wrestling careers back to back. I looked at my old teammate and said, "This is like a punch in the gut."

"No doubt," Todd responded.

It was so frustrating to watch Dakota lose to two boys that I thought he was better than. No one wants to see their high school career end like that. However, truth be told, Dakota is really only a second-year wrestler. And for him to even be at the Connecticut State Open Tournament is a significant accomplishment on its own. We are all proud of him. And he should be proud of himself too. Furthermore, the Waterford boy Dakota lost to 5-1 the previous weekend took 2nd at the Connecticut State Open. To only lose 5-1 to the second-best kid in Connecticut is an amazing feat!

Sadly, my 126-pounder and heavyweight lost their next two matches, and they were out of the tournament too. Like Dakota, they both wrestled courageously, and the matches were close, but they both still lost. Fortunately, neither one is a senior, and they are both coming back next year. And maybe next year, they'll both get a crack at the New England's.

Dakota has worked very hard over his high school wrestling career. He has learned a lot and has excellent technique. I, too, have worked very hard helping him become a better wrestler. However, at this moment, I am painfully pondering on what I could have done differently to have better prepared him. At this moment, I'm not sure what I could have done differently. Dakota is probably not sure either. However, I am sure that Dakota did something very hard, which is to have wrestled in high school. And in that process, he has gained some character. And I believe that that is what I was looking for... the making of a good young man.

Brian Preece: Though Dakota came up short of his goal of being a state champion, I congratulate him for being a wrestler. He took that journey into what I think is the toughest sport a young person can do. It's not just the physical demands of the sport, but as I said before, you are alone when you're out on the mat. There are no teammates out there with you, your coach is in the corner, and everyone in the stands sees who won or lost. Even in other individual sports, you can sometimes "hide" among a sea of competitors. But when you are out there on the mat, whether it's in a dual meet or the state championship match, all eyes are on you. It's not a place for the faint of heart.

I think there were many things out of Dakota's control. I have coached state champions and state placers that started the sport a little later in life, like Dakota. But because of injuries and COVID-19, Dakota really lost two complete seasons of experience. And in the middleweights, that is really hard to overcome. And during a lot of his freshman season and some of his senior year, he fought injuries. And even in this last year, COVID-19 and some bad weather events took even more valuable mat time away from Dakota. Yet, Dakota won his fair share of matches. He earned the respect of his teammates and coaches by being named a team captain. And left it all out there on the mat, even in his final defeats. In the last chapter of this book, we will learn how wrestling changed Dakota's life for the better, and he's well on his way to becoming a good man.

My own Dad had this analogy of what wrestling did for the individual. He said your life was like a gallon bucket of water. And wrestling was like a drop of food coloring. When you put that drop of food coloring in the larger bucket of water, it gives it color. The gallon of water is forever changed by that one drop of food coloring. Though one can spend a lot of time as it seems wrestling, the time wrestling in the big scheme of things is just a tiny portion of one's life. Like Daniel and I have, I think Dakota will find out that being a wrestler is one of the most important decisions he ever made.

It doesn't mean that Dakota or Daniel will not have regret or sadness that the journey ended short of the ultimate goal. Any competitor (wrestler or coach) worth their salt wants to win. We crave victory, and defeat is difficult for us to bear.

I remember months after coming up short of taking state my senior year. I had my lowest moment of despair, even worse than right after the match; quite frankly, when I was working at my job in the dairy department of Dan's Foods. I was having a bad night, and I remember being in the cooler screaming at God that life was unfair, that I had spent years in this sport, and I didn't take state. I made a game effort to take state, and in my matches at state, I lay it out on the line. I also learned that my Dad was proud of what I accomplished. I didn't let him down. He coached dozens of state champions, and I wanted to be one of those. It didn't happen, but he still loved me. But for a while, coming up short was painful, and I had to wrestle (pardon the pun) with how to deal with what life handed me as an 18-year-old senior.

I even think now that me not taking state was a blessing. Learning from that disappointment, I believe, has given me empathy to relate to the wrestlers that I coached that might have their own seasons end in disappointment. It was the hand that I was dealt, so one has to live with it, and maybe not just live with it, but use your life experiences to help others. That's what I've tried to do.

Writing these books with Daniel has been a lot of fun as it has caused me to reflect on my life in wrestling. It has brought back memories of wrestling for my Dad and later as a coach. I thank Dakota for taking this journey in wrestling and his experience being the vehicle that brought Daniel and me together to write these three wrestling books. I hope people will read and reread them because I think there are important lessons in them. When Dakota started wrestling, none of us knew where the journey would end. None of us knew that he would only lose 5-1 to that Waterford kid who took 2nd at the State Open.

I can't say thanks enough to my wife, Heidi, who has given up a lot of time with me as I pursued my coaching life. Even when I gave up my position as a full-time head coach, I remained very involved in wrestling in different roles. I kept coaching baseball, football, and golf, along with a two-year return as a full-time assistant wrestling coach. She kept the home front in order as she worked a full-time job as department chair in Special Education. I thank my children Lizzy and Zach for their love and support and ask for some forgiveness for spending a lot of time with other people's children at their expense. Additionally, Heidi's parents Bob and Janet Stone, deserve praise. They were often visitors to our home during my coaching days and did many things to help us around the house and tending children.

As I think about my wife Heidi's sacrifices, I better realize the sacrifices of my own mother. When you are younger, you don't notice these things. It wasn't until I was older that I realized how much time my Mom spent taking care of us while my Dad was away. It seemed like he was always at meets or holding both high school practices followed by youth practices until late into the night. When my Dad was in his heyday, Mom took care of three young children. My Mom is a tough cookie, and oftentimes she was the one that would give me the advice or counsel I needed to hear even though it might not have been what I wanted to hear. And by the time this final book is published, my Mom would have lived the last 25 years without her husband, who died too young at age 57. I know that has been tough for her, but she has supported her children and grandchildren in their endeavors. She has been generous in many ways to our family.

There are so many people to thank in my village of life and wrestling. One person that was a significant influence was my junior high coach in 7th grade, Dan Leatherwood. Coach Leatherwood was basically assigned to coach wrestling but was really a basketball coach and a good one. He would lead one of his high school teams to a runner-up finish later in his coaching career. He didn't know much about wrestling, but he knew a lot about coaching, and he inspired me. I won the District championship, and I owe a lot to him. My other junior high coaches, Carl Bennett in 8th grade and Dick Robbins in 9th grade, were also good men and good examples.

When I went to high school, I was first coached by Alan Albright in my sophomore year. He would also coach me a year in college at BYU, and then we would coach against each other when I became a coach. He was also a counselor at the high school where my wife worked for several years. But I remember how he made wrestling a bit more fun for me when I needed it to be fun. We have remained friends over the years.

Though I wrestled in teams that were few in number, I had some good teammates that inspired me and made me a better wrestler including 2X state champion and All-American John Robbins and state champ Chris Whitney. Others that inspired me as a younger high school wrestler were state placers Tim Clark and Chad Gallager, along with Chris Barton, one of my team captains my junior year. Throughout all three years I wrestled with Perry Benally and state champ Jon Clark. And joining my team my junior season was my primary workout partner Mark Hult, along with J John Suprise who only wrestled one year in high school and nearly placed in state. In my senior year, move-in Bryan Dayton became a good friend and we had three deaf athletes, two of which stuck with it, Lyle Monsen and Layne Owens, join our team and they were truly remarkable individuals. Again, all part of my village, making me either a better wrestler directly and certainly a better man with their friendship and mentorship.

I also want to single out one of my Dad's assistant coaches, Leonard Garcia, who remains a close friend today. My Dad and I had some rough moments, but he was there for me and helped me do what I needed to do to smooth things over.

I had other important mentors in my life, such as Clarann Jacobs (Mrs. J as she was called). She was my journalism teacher and such an outstanding and caring teacher. I was pulled into two possible career directions, journalism and teaching/coaching. Though teaching and coaching paid my bills, I kept writing sports stories and other things. She is buried close to my father's crypt, and I regularly try to visit both their resting places to give them thanks.

Our high school football coach Ray Groth was another influential figure. I didn't play a down of football but helped out as a statistician, and then in the off-season for both football and wrestling, he opened up the weight room and gave me both great life advice and helped me to be stronger and fitter. I had great Boy Scout leaders like Richard Fowles and Joe Mills, who were great role models outside of wrestling. Another critical father figure to me was one of my bosses at Dan's Foods, Bob Duzett. He reinforced the importance of a strong work ethic.

When I went to BYU, I made good friends like Lee Dorsett, Erik Holdaway, Doug Koob, Bill Morris, Mark Smith, Chris Weston, Laurie Hilton, and her family. All had a good influence on me. My friend Doug went into hotel management and allowed several of my teams to stay at his hotels at very good rates. My friend Lee, like me, went into teaching and coaching and became a football, girls' soccer, and wrestling coach, and a good one at that. He has told me many times about my father's influence on him. My father told him he could be a successful coach in any sport, regardless of whether he had experience in it. As my father often told him, "a good coach can coach anything." I coached many youth baseball teams with my friend Erik, who knows more sports history than anyone I know. He has a great analytical mind, and along with Darren, who I consider my closest friend besides my wife, Heidi. I also had two great professors in Dr. D. Michael Quinn and Dr. Garn Coombs.

I want to mention the love and support of Uncle Emery and Aunt Carol Schattinger. They were educators and some of the most positive, kind people I know. I know there were times when they were sounding boards for me on the big decisions in my life.

When I coached youth baseball, I was blessed to coach alongside some great men like Gene Bechthold, a tremendous influence on my younger brother Scott. And while I coached some of his sons (Tyler and Ryan), Dick Geertsen (and his entire family) were great friends. His oldest son Jeff was one of my assistant coaches when we won a state title. Before the final championship game, Dick gave me some great advice that helped me lead the team to victory.

I want to thank Gary Roylance, who gave me my first official high school coaching job as a college-intern assistant coach at Provo High School. Then my college teammate Jess Christen took over the next year, and I carried on with him. And then Jess called me up and convinced me to come back to Provo High School and try my hand at being the head coach.

But the five years between my assistant and then head coaching experiences at Provo High School, I worked at West High School. I cherish my time there, where I coached alongside a great man in Don Holtry, who again taught me the day-to-day operations of being a head coach. He allowed me to take the stage a lot and shape our program, for which I was grateful, genuinely preparing me for my head coaching gig. While I was there, I got to work with other awesome people like Dan Potts and Steve Cardon. As I struggled to learn the craft of being a classroom teacher, I had some great mentors from Connie Jeanne Larsen, Gene Lynch, Sharon Pittam, and Kathryn Romney, who helped me survive those early years.

When I came to Provo High School, I was blessed to work with great people. First and foremost, I need to thank my right-hand man Darren Hirsche. He assisted me for 10 years in wrestling, and we worked together in football, as well. We both taught in the Social Studies department. We spent hours talking about teaching, coaching, and life, going on several road trips together, and spending many days on the golf course. But then Huntington's disease took my best friend's life at age 52, and I miss him dearly.

I also want to call out Dr. Stephen Oliverson, one of the assistant principals, when I was hired. He was a tremendous support to our program and remained a good friend. Other great support and friendship came from Cesar Cardoso, Margaret Craft, Marge Hutchings, Jennifer Hyde (Young), and Todd Smith—all members of the original Spirit Club with Darren and me. Marge and Margaret plotted to bring Heidi and me together. Cesar was our athletic director, while I was his assistant for a time, and Todd was another close friend and colleague in both the teaching and coaching ranks. There were many other faculty and staff that were top shelf. Thanks Colette (Thomas) for your long suffering patience with me as I learned the ropes of state, district, and school fiscal policy.

I got to coach with two great head coaches in Vance Law and Lance Moore in baseball. Both were good to me and taught me a lot about coaching and leading young men. I generally want to say thanks to all the administrators and their office staff for their support and letting me host some of the events I did at Provo High School and doing the things that made my life as a teacher and coach a bit easier. I know I'm forgetting many people in which I ask for some grace. I also had so many great assistant coaches, especially those Blevin brothers Chad and Travis. I would like to thank Chris Miller, who assisted me one year, and then was my successor, for allowing me to be a part of the program on my own terms years after. And the other two head coaches after Chris, Austin Frazier and Mike Olsen, who allowed me to keep doing the Wrestling Against Cancer Duals. I am also excited that one of my former wrestlers, Gerrit Greer, has just been named the new head coach beginning next year and I might be stepping up my involvement in the program. And I also worked with some good people in the football program.

Of course, I want to thank the wrestlers I coached that took the journey with me. Some became state champions and placers. Others hardly won a match, but no matter, thanks for giving it a try. Some became assistant coaches with me like Jason Finlinson, David Nielson, Patrick Porter, Kyle Thompson, Sean Walker, Braeden Woodger, and Greg Wright. With Greg, he was there when my friend Darren took a couple of years leave, and he took on a lot as an assistant coach while also coaching the junior high team. He now is one of the best officials in the state. Braeden has become a great family friend. He helps me run tournaments and has done a lot of construction around my houses, including finishing our basement at our current residence. Of course, many of my wrestlers had awesome parents who helped our program in so many ways. Too many to mention, but thanks!

I also truly appreciate my friendship with Andy Unsicker. I got to know him as a vendor, but then for the last two decades, I've helped him out with his big youth tournament. He loves wrestling, especially Iowa Hawkeye wrestling, like no other. He has a crowned tooth with the Hawkeye logo to prove it. We have traveled to some NCAA tournaments together, and, as I said, he took care of our program needs in regards to gear, medals, plaques, and trophies for years. His wife Natalie and the rest of his family are simply fantastic people.

My own siblings were great examples of success. My younger brother Scott was a state champion wrestler and great baseball player, and like me, dabbled a bit in golf. I coached him a lot, especially baseball, and I cherish those times. Then we coached an American Legion baseball team together, which was a blast. Born over two months premature, it's really a miracle he's even with us. He struggled in his early life and had a good chunk of his intestine removed. He's a shining example of perseverance. I also appreciated when he would drop by and show some moves and share his wisdom with my wrestlers.

My sister Deanna is arguably even a better coach than my father. She didn't win as many state titles but won state titles at two different schools and six total in volleyball. She was a 4-sport athlete in high school. She was the pesky little sister who followed me around a lot and would mix it up with the boys in any sport we played. She won nearly 500 games as a coach. Now she'll retire after a great career as a volleyball coach, winning those six state titles along with four runner-up finishes and 12 times taking her teams to the final four. I remember a lot of great phone calls where we shared advice with each other.

It might sound strange, but I want to thank some of my best rivals on the mat, both as a wrestler and a coach. Over time, we have learned what Larry Bird meant to Magic Johnson and vice versa. I had opponents that pushed me and helped me become a better wrestler. I think there is a unique camaraderie between wrestlers and wrestling coaches that doesn't exist in other sports. I mean, how can I not mention Pat Bradshaw of Granger High who I wrestled five times my senior year or what was 20 percent of my matches.

All of us have a village that helped us get to where we are. My village was truly enormous, and I feel blessed that way. And of course, there was my father. It's hard to describe him. He was a larger-than-life figure who I tried, and failed miserably, to measure up with. But he wasn't perfect, and our relationship wasn't perfect. Quite frankly, many of my cherished memories of him were away from the wrestling mat. It wasn't easy being a son of a famous wrestling coach. Yet in the big scheme of things, no regrets.

Lastly, I think Dakota will someday look back at this journey he took very fondly. He will truly cherish those drives home from practice with Daniel as they conversed about wrestling and life. Perhaps Dakota's journey in wrestling isn't quite over. I hope this is just the beginning of a long journey in the sport. Maybe he'll officiate, coach, or find some other ways to give back. But thanks again, Dakota, for becoming a wrestler. You gave your Dad and me a chance to forge our own friendship and author these books.

Chapter 14

IN DAKOTA'S OWN WORDS

This is the week of the New England Wrestling Championships. None of our E.O. Smith wrestlers qualified for this elite-level U.S. northeastern tournament. However, Connecticut wrestlers did do well. Saint John's Prep of Danvers, Massachusetts, took the team title. But, Xavier High School from Connecticut took second.

From Connecticut, Killingly's Jack Richardson (145), Fairfield Warde's Will Ebert (170), and Guilford's Chris Murphy (195) each won New England titles while Xavier's Jackson Heslin (120), New Milford's Evan Lindner (126), Simsbury's Zach Jones (152) and Norwalk's Brendan Gilchrist (195) each finished second. Both finalists at the 195-pound weight class were both from Connecticut. And four of the top ten teams in the New England's were from Connecticut.

I wish Dakota had gotten a chance to wrestle in the New England's. But he didn't. And I fully understand that he just didn't have enough mat time to earn his way there. And that's okay because our mission was always about building character and becoming a good man instead of just winning trophies.

After four years, it looks like this might be my last piece of writing on Dakota's high school wrestling career. I remember when this day seemed so far away. I can't thank enough the New York Times Bestselling Author Scott Schulte, who wrote the Dan Gable story, A Wrestling Life, for his support and encouragement in this endeavor. Scott also introduced me to Brian Preece. Brian became my co-author of our trilogy of wrestling books, starting with, *Hitting the Mat* based on my son Dakota's high school wrestling experience.

Brian Preece is an amazing man, and we complimented each other nicely. As a former champion, I am the father and wrestling coach of my son, Dakota. Brian was the son of a legendary wrestling coach who had never wrestled before. I am an East Coast progressive New Englander from the tiny state of Connecticut. Brian is a little more of a conservative Westerner from the large state of Utah. And Brian is about a decade older than me. He has really opened my eyes to how excellent Utah wrestling is and how cutting edge they are, too, with their female wrestling program. We're both very different during these politically divisive times in our country's history. But we're also way more alike than different. We are both wrestlers, athletes, coaches, teachers, authors, columnists, public speakers, husbands and fathers, and the list goes on and on... We're both good men who respect each other and want the best for each other. We also want the best for every athlete and athlete's family out there, especially if they wrestle.

Thanks, Brian Preece. My world has been much enriched with you in it. I look forward to us being on more podcast shows together in the future, having a great time talking about wrestling.

Lastly, my son Dakota gave me a real gift when he entered high school and decided to try wrestling. He brought me back into a world that I loved and missed dearly, wrestling. I saw more old friends over the last four years than I could count. I actually got to be my son's high school wrestling coach. How many fathers get to do that? Not many! I felt useful and very proud helping Dakota, and his teammates become good young men.

And I think I successfully completed my mission of being a good man who raises a good man to replace himself someday. Look below at the high school senior essay project that Dakota wrote on the benefits of wrestling. Maybe Dakota didn't win States or go to the New England's. But it looks like his potential is unlimited as you read below and notice how he emphasizes a growth mindset. I'm so proud of him!

Dakota's Thoughts on the Benefits of Wrestling

Sports have always been inherently beneficial since the beginning of time, whether it's to improve physical fitness, meet new people, develop new skills, or even just have fun. Sports can also teach youth-specific values to have a higher likelihood of succeeding in life. Wrestling is no exception. While wrestling is assuredly a daunting challenge for newcomers, it is also one of the most rewarding sports. The youth is taught through wrestling how to face challenges head-on and come out on top. **The sport of wrestling effectively teaches the youth the life lessons and values needed to succeed later in life.**

One of many priceless lessons that adolescents need to learn to thrive in the real world is to persevere. Perseverance is all about getting up and trying again when a failure occurs. Likewise, anybody who is successful in their respected field knows that one must learn from their accumulated failures to succeed. Wrestling is a tremendously difficult sport, and it teaches young wrestlers that failure is just an opportunity for growth. Whether it's learning new moves, taking risks during matches, making weight, or overcoming injuries, it requires a lot of perseverance to improve in wrestling. And there are many opportunities to fail. According to the article "Values Learned in Youth Wrestling" by Matt Krumrie, "Wrestling teaches the importance of "if at first, you don't succeed, try, try again. Through wrestling, they have learned that if they continue to work on their failures, they can eventually get it—and achieve success" (Krumrie). The sport of wrestling empowers the youth by giving praise through their efforts instead of their results. When kids are taught to focus on their efforts instead of their results, it gives them a sense of control over their lives. And it improves their confidence. In real-world terms, it could be getting fired from a job, being evicted from their homes, making a poor first impression on your boss, or not getting the raise you know you deserve. For many, these setbacks could mean the end of the world. But wrestlers understand that these setbacks are an opportunity for growth. The article "Advantages of Wrestling Competitions for Children" by legendsmma.net states that "To succeed in a local wrestling competition and build discipline, children need to develop certain habits. For example, they have to wake up early, eat a balanced diet for their desired weight, and at times sacrifice their social life to compete. Sometimes they even have to do tasks that seem to be impossible for them to achieve" (legendsmma.net).

This is especially important because those who stick with wrestling and see improvements in themselves can develop a growth mindset. A growth mindset is imperative towards achieving success in whatever goals are desired. A growth mindset allows one to acknowledge they can develop their skills through effort, versus a fixed mindset which believes that abilities and skills are set in stone. The similarity between a growth mindset and perseverance is that they are often interchangeable. A child who displays a growth mindset acknowledges that they can grow and improve at whatever they set their mind to. A child who demonstrates perseverance often puts their best effort forth to strive for success no matter the obstacles or setbacks. Both perseverance and a growth mindset are about accepting failure to be part of the process and striving for growth and improvement in their corresponding fields.

Another important value that adolescents are taught in wrestling is discipline. Discipline is not only about following rules but about setting higher standards for oneself. It's about the behaviors and actions that one will and won't accept from themselves. Discipline is needed to build beneficial habits that will improve chances of success and quality of life. Being exceptional is difficult, while being mediocre is easy. Actions and behaviors directly influence the outcome of lives as well as performance. In wrestling, discipline is a necessity. Youth wrestlers learn to push themselves during practice. Eat a healthier and more balanced diet, manage their time between practice and school. And put in extra work when nobody else does.

Discipline also coincides with responsibility. When kids learn to take responsibility for themselves and their actions, they learn how to be independent and be motivated by their desire to improve. In an article by the name of "Why Kids Should Wrestle" by theschoolofwrestling.com, the piece expresses that "As an individual sport, the only person responsible for success or failure in wrestling is the individual themselves. Wrestling teaches self-awareness and how to be responsible for your own actions. What you put in is what you get out" (theschoolofwrestling.com). Responsibility is a critical lesson for kids to learn that will support them throughout their lives. Not only does responsibility correlate with wrestling, but in many real-life situations. When the youth can cultivate and learn responsibility, the skill seeps into other aspects of their lives. They learn to take responsibility for their schoolwork, their chores at home, their behavior, and the small choices they make throughout their day. A perfect example of a wrestler taking responsibility for their actions is to make healthier food choices to maximize their wrestling performance and achieve their desired weight class. Discipline is a skill that benefits lives in an infinite number of ways. Young wrestlers who practice discipline learn that they ultimately control their destiny. The website Ciscoathletic.com expresses in their article "Benefits of Youth Wrestling," "if you want to win, you have to be disciplined. You need to make sure you are following a routine to keep your body fit and provide yourself with the energy to perform. It involves keeping to a strict diet and avoiding unhealthy junk food. As such, it teaches kids to look after their body and themselves, as well as ensuring that they learn the importance of following the rules" (ciscoathlete.com). Learning how to nurture a healthy, balanced, and nutritional diet will ultimately benefit many facets of the youth's lives. When discipline is developed, adolescents learn how to make better choices and decisions for their future selves.

The third and final value that wrestling develops in the youth (although there are too many to count) is confidence. Confidence is all about being self-assured and believing in one's abilities. Funnily enough, one can have the skills needed and still lack the confidence to execute these skills. Young wrestlers learn to build confidence by putting in the work required to succeed. When wrestlers push themselves and give 100% of their effort, they are inherently confident because they have done all the work they possibly could have. Losing is a part of life, and wrestling is no exception. However, adolescents learn to still be satisfied with themselves, even if they lost, because they had given their all. Not only does this confidence present itself in the sport of wrestling, but in social interactions with other athletes as well. This can be especially useful growing up because communication is essential in life. As maintained by "The Social Benefits of Wrestling" by teamusa.org, "kids from around the country exchange singlets with kids they've never met before. Sure, some may be quick conversations, but at some point, these young athletes had to muster the courage to speak to what is, in most cases, a stranger. These experiences are providing building blocks for future communications, such as in that first job interview, during an interview for a scholarship from a community organization, or even in the classroom setting, where many kids don't feel comfortable raising their hand and asking questions in front of others" (teamusa.org). Wrestling can be an opportunity for many juveniles to travel to places they've never been before and practice interacting with new people as well as making new friendships. Over time, confidence grows.

The skill of confidence can offer an abundance of advantages within an adolescent's life, including performance, communication, self-esteem, reduced anxiety, and mindset. Confidence prepares young wrestlers for life and its many unpredictable challenges. Following the previous article "The Advantages of Wrestling Competitions for Children" by legendsmma.net, "In competitions, kids are accountable for both their successes and failures. Therefore they need to be highly confident. Without an optimistic attitude, success can elude them. From the beginning, children learn to count on themselves and gain confidence on and off the wrestling mat." (legendsmma.net). Due to the difficulty of wrestling, it is quite common to attempt and accomplish hard things daily. This is a great way for young wrestlers to build self-confidence.

In short, the sport of wrestling consistently and effectively teaches young wrestlers the skills and values they require to succeed in life. There are countless lessons taught throughout wrestling. Perseverance aids adolescents in pushing through and overcoming obstacles set in front of them and developing a growth mindset. Discipline gives service by guiding juveniles on being responsible for themselves and taking the actions needed to achieve their goals. Lastly, confidence is everything. Those who are self-assured and unconditionally believe in themselves can accomplish whatever they set their mind to. Wrestling is more than just a sport. For different people, wrestling can be anything. It could be a way to make new friends. Or an outlet for adverse circumstances in life, a way to set and achieve goals, have fun, improve health and fitness, bond with family members, and the list goes on. The sport of wrestling has been here since the beginning of time. It has guided millions of people throughout the game we call life, and it won't be going anywhere anytime soon.

Dakota Blanchard
All-Academic
All-Conference
Team MVP

ABOUT THE AUTHORS

Dan Blanchard: Bestselling and Award-Winning, Author, Speaker, and Educator. TV Host. Two-time Junior Olympian Wrestler and two-time Junior Olympian Wrestling Coach who grew up as a student-athlete. However, Dan admits that as a youth he was more of an athlete than a student. Dan has now successfully completed fourteen years of college and has earned seven degrees. He teaches Special Education and Social Studies in Connecticut's largest inner-city high school where he was chosen by the AFT-CT as the face and voice of educational reform and is now on the speaking circuit for them. Dan was with the team that put forth Connecticut's new Social Studies Frameworks and is also a member of the Special Education Advisory Board to the Connecticut State Department of Education. In addition, Dan is a Teacher Consultant for the University of Connecticut's Writing Project. Finally, Dan is a double veteran of the Army and the Air Force. Find out more about Dan and his other books: www.DanBlanchard.net.

Brian Preece: He can't really remember a time when he wasn't involved in the sport of wrestling. His father Dennis, a Hall of Fame wrestling coach from the State of Utah, introduced

Brian to the sport at a young age in the early 1970s. As a competitor, Brian won a state freestyle championship and was a 2-time region (league) champion, as well as a 2-time state placer in high school. He wrestled one year at Brigham Young University before embarking on a teaching and coaching career that spanned over 30 years. As a coach, he was recognized as the 2006 Utah Coach of the Year by the National Wrestling Coaches Association. Besides coaching, Brian also was an official, event organizer, and an early benefactor to the Utah Valley University wrestling program. But he is perhaps best known in Utah wrestling circles for the media coverage and historical perspective he has brought to the sport for parts of five decades. By joining forces with author Daniel Blanchard, the two hope to bring a fresh perspective of the father-son dynamic that is truly unique to the sport of wrestling. Brian currently resides in Mapleton, Utah, and with his wife, Heidi, and are the proud parents of two adult children (Lizzy age 22, and Zach age 20).

OTHER BOOKS BY DAN AND BRIAN

HITTING THE MAT

The Making of a State Champion
or At Least a Good Man!

"I know you're going to be inspired by this book. It's a rare look inside the sport of wrestling."
Dan Gable

DAN BLANCHARD & BRIAN PREECE

*Take a FREE peek inside, *Hitting the Mat*:
https://tinyurl.com/y9jf37mp

TRYING TO TAKE THE MAT

*The Making of a State Champ
or At Least a Good Man*

DAN BLANCHARD & BRIAN PREECE

*Take a FREE peek inside, *Trying to Take the Mat*:
https://tinyurl.com/4fv9vea3

PICTURES OF DAKOTA'S HIGH SCHOOL WRESTLING CAREER

KT KIDZ Fall 9th grade

9th grade E.O. Smith Wrestling Team

10th grade with injured knee

11th grade basement wrestling mat bought with Covid funds.

Dakota 12th grade

Dakota with another victory

Dakota 12th grade, and his dad Dan

Co-author Brian Preece with his sister Deanna Meyer who recently announced her retirement as a teacher and head volleyball coach. Meyer won six state titles at two different schools and won league titles at three different schools following success-fully in the footsteps of her father Dennis Preece who coached 10 state titles at Unitas High School in wrestling and golf.

Brian Preece with one of his former assistant coaches Travis Blevins. Travis' son Tyler placed third in 4A state in 2022.

Brian Preece with three of his former wrestlers from Provo High School. From L-R, Trent Beesley. Gerrit Greer and Shawn Por-ter. Greer was recently hired as the new head coach at the school.

Co-author Brian Preece with one his former wrestlers Greg Wright, who is also a top high school official in Utah. Wright also served as Preece's assistant coach for several years.

Co-author Brian Preece with his wife of 25 years Heidi.

Co-author Brian Preece with twin brothers Travis (L) and Chad (R). Chad was the former head coach at Mountain View High School, now assisting, while Travis serves as a youth coach in the community.

L-R Darren Hirsche, longtime assistant coach to co/author Brian Preece; Scott Preece, younger brother to Brian Preece and 1991 4A 145-pound state champion; Brian Preece

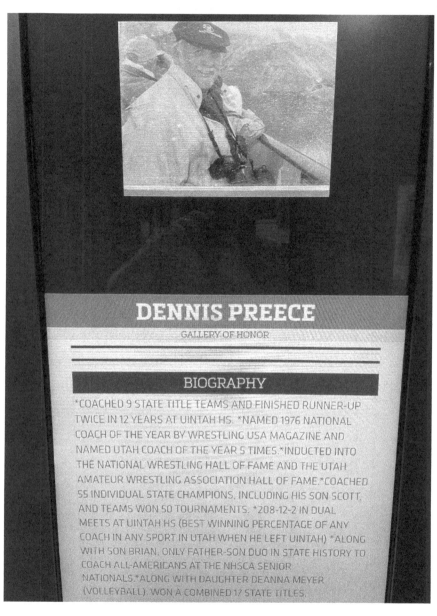

DENNIS PREECE

GALLERY OF HONOR

BIOGRAPHY

*COACHED 9 STATE TITLE TEAMS AND FINISHED RUNNER-UP TWICE IN 12 YEARS AT UINTAH HS. *NAMED 1976 NATIONAL COACH OF THE YEAR BY WRESTLING USA MAGAZINE AND NAMED UTAH COACH OF THE YEAR 5 TIMES.*INDUCTED INTO THE NATIONAL WRESTLING HALL OF FAME AND THE UTAH AMATEUR WRESTLING ASSOCIATION HALL OF FAME.*COACHED 55 INDIVIDUAL STATE CHAMPIONS, INCLUDING HIS SON SCOTT, AND TEAMS WON 50 TOURNAMENTS. *208-12-2 IN DUAL MEETS AT UINTAH HS (BEST WINNING PERCENTAGE OF ANY COACH IN ANY SPORT IN UTAH WHEN HE LEFT UINTAH) *ALONG WITH SON BRIAN, ONLY FATHER-SON DUO IN STATE HISTORY TO COACH ALL-AMERICANS AT THE NHSCA SENIOR NATIONALS.*ALONG WITH DAUGHTER DEANNA MEYER (VOLLEYBALL), WON A COMBINED 17 STATE TITLES.

Brian Preece's dad, Dennis Preece, photo and biography at the Utah Sports Hall of Fame.

Made in USA - Kendallville, IN
39365_9781737253525
07.07.2022 1330